GUTS & GLORY

THE VIKINGS

GUTS & GLORY

THE VIKINGS

BEN THOMPSON

ILLUSTRATIONS BY

C. M. BUTZER

Little, Brown and Company

New York   Boston

Little, Brown and Company

Hachette Book Group
1290 Avenue of the Americas, New York, NY 10104
Visit us at lb-kids.com

Little, Brown and Company is a division of Hachette Book Group, Inc.
The Little, Brown name and logo are trademarks of Hachette Book Group, Inc.

The publisher is not responsible for websites (or their content) that are not owned by the publisher.

First Edition: June 2015

Library of Congress Cataloging-in-Publication Data

Thompson, Ben, 1980–
Guts & glory : the Vikings / Ben Thompson ; Illustrations by C. M. Butzer. — First edition.
pages cm
Includes bibliographical references and index.
ISBN 978-0-316-32056-6 (hardcover) — ISBN 978-0-316-32055-9 (ebook) — ISBN 978-0-316-32198-3 (library edition ebook) 1. Vikings—Juvenile literature. 2. Civilization, Viking—Juvenile literature. I. Butzer, C. M., illustrator. II. Title.
DL65.T36 2015
948'.022—dc23
2014025217

10 9 8 7 6 5 4 3 2

RRD-C

Printed in the United States of America

Image Credits:
Courtesy of Tasnu Arakun: runic alphabet, page 81
Courtesy of Erik Brate: rune stone, page 81
Courtesy of Detroit Publishing Company/US Library of Congress: page 250

CATTLE DIE, KINSMEN DIE,
EACH MAN DIES HIMSELF.

BUT FAME NEVER DIES
FOR ANYONE WHO WINS
A GOOD NAME.

—Viking proverb

CONTENTS

Deliver us, O Lord,
from the Fury of the Norsemen.

—Ninth-century Catholic prayer

Introduction 1

Author's Note 4

1. The Viking Warrior 9

One of the most feared fighters in the history of the world, a typical Viking is two hundred pounds of muscle packed into a suit of chain mail armor and set loose with a battle-axe. No bigs.

2. Norse Mythology 29

From Thor's hammer to an epic war between gods and monsters, the religion of the Vikings isn't the sort of thing you'd expect to learn at Sunday school.

3. Turgeis the Devil 44

The fact that this ferocious sea-raider founded Dublin doesn't save him from being the most hated Norseman in the history of Ireland.

4. The Voyage of Hasting 59

After crossing swords with Moorish warriors in North Africa, a wide-ranging Viking duo heads across the Mediterranean and lays waste to Italy.

5. Kievan Rus 73

The amazing true tale of how the Vikings inadvertently found modern-day Russia.

6. The Vikings at Home 83

When most Northmen aren't raiding, marauding, and killing, they enjoy eating salted fish, drowning one another in lakes, and watching horses fight to the death.

7. The Great Heathen Army 96

Seeking to avenge his murdered father, the awesomely named Viking lord Ivar the Boneless leads the largest armada of warships England has ever seen across the North Sea in a full-scale invasion.

8. Britain Fights Back 108

Smashed on the battlefield and forced to flee into the dark marshes of Britain, a young English prince named Alfred swears to retake his homeland from the invading hordes.

9. Harald Fairhair 121

After a girl makes fun of his puny little kingdom, Harald Fairhair decides he's not going to cut his hair until he's conquered all of Norway. And that's what he does.

10. Gunnhild, Mother of Kings 134

A devoted wife, fierce mother, and vengeance-hungry warrior, the bloodthirsty "Mother of Kings" is one of the most hated, capable, and influential women in Norwegian history.

11. The Siege of Paris 150

When the heathens come knocking on the gates of the City of Love, a defiant Frankish count responds by dumping a vat of boiling-hot oil on their heads.

12. Hrolf the Walker 163

One plunder-seeking warrior's journey from frothing-at-the-mouth Viking to iron-fisted European nobleman.

13. Egil Skallagrimsson 175

Vikings are so tough that even their world-renowned poets have a startling tendency to cleave their enemies in two with an axe.

14. Saint Olga of Kiev 188

Taking over the throne of Russia after the untimely demise of her husband, this fearsome warrior-queen avenges him with extreme, fiery violence. Then she becomes a saint.

15. Erik the Red 201

A semipsychotic convicted murderer discovers Greenland, realizes it's basically uninhabitable, then inexplicably persuades a couple hundred people to follow him there and let him rule as their king.

16. The Varangian Guard 213

Known alternately as "axe-bearing foreigners" and "the emperor's wine-bags," this ferocious unit of Viking mercenaries defends the Eastern Roman Empire for centuries.

17. Christianity Comes to Heathendom 225

The most revered of all the sword-swinging Viking rulers, the legendary Olaf Crowbone baptizes his people in the most Viking way possible—by angrily threatening them with extreme bodily harm.

18. The Vikings Discover America 240

Leif the Lucky undertakes a daring sea voyage and amazingly discovers the New World five centuries before Christopher Columbus.

19. The Decline and Fall of Ethelred the Unready 252

When King Ethelred of England orders the slaughter of all Vikings in England, he foolishly fails to anticipate the lengths to which Vikings will go for vengeance— which is why we now know him as Ethelred the Unready.

20. The Norman Conquest 264

The Viking Age comes to an end with an epoch-changing three-way showdown for ultimate control of the English crown, and Europe will never be the same again.

Conclusion 276

Acknowledgments 279

Bibliography 281

Index 285

INTRODUCTION

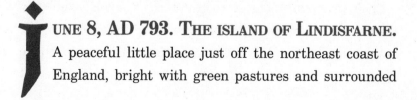

THE COMING OF THE NORSEMEN

And they came to the Church of Lindisfarne, laid everything waste with grievous plundering, trampled the holy places with polluted steps, dug up the altars and seized all the treasures of the holy church. They killed some of the brothers, took some away with them in fetters, many they drove out, naked and loaded with insults, some they drowned in the sea.

—The Anglo-Saxon Chronicle

JUNE 8, AD 793. THE ISLAND OF LINDISFARNE. A peaceful little place just off the northeast coast of England, bright with green pastures and surrounded on all sides by the rolling waves of the North Sea. At the Monastery of Saint Cuthbert, a few dozen Catholic monks dutifully tended to their chores or offered prayers in the breathtaking chapel.

Then from the east appeared an unusual sight. At the very edge of vision were two strange-looking ships approaching from a direction from which ships didn't typically approach. Quietly, quickly, these small, fast-moving vessels made their way toward the island, each powered by a single red-and-white sail and sixty oars.

By the time the citizens could make out the black, ornately carved dragon heads glaring menacingly from the prows and see the glistening muscles of the heavily armored men rowing toward them, it was already too late.

The terrifying sea-raiders struck so fast that many of the monks didn't have time to hide their valuables. With blood-curdling battle cries, a swarm of humongous bearded warriors tore through the island, slaughtering and burning and throwing people out windows as monks and pilgrims ran for their lives. Those who weren't killed were captured, bound in ropes, and dragged back to the ships as captives, never to be heard from again.

The ravagers made straight for the chapel, completely unaware of its religious importance. They took gold crosses, silver cups and candlesticks, and ivory chests. They tore jeweled covers from Bibles, pried gems from walls, ripped priceless silk tapestries, and torched buildings.

They departed just as quickly as they'd arrived, leaving behind a smoldering wake of burning cinders and charred rubble. None of the ruined survivors knew anything about where the mysterious men had come from, what they wanted, or where they were headed. Those monks unlucky enough to witness the anarchy believed it was a scourge sent by God to punish humanity for its sins.

For the next three hundred years, these fearsome raiders would plague the lands of Europe. They'd be known by many different titles—the Norse, the Ashmen, the Northmen, and the Danes—but one name in particular has stood throughout time:

The Vikings.

AUTHOR'S NOTE

> Sometimes it's not possible to know every word and every happening, for most things happen long before they're told about.
>
> —The Saga of Hrolf the Walker

FROM ESPN HIGHLIGHTS OF MINNESOTA Vikings running backs trampling linebackers to *How to Train Your Dragon* movie marathons, we can feel the influence of the Vikings in almost every aspect of our daily lives. Sometimes those influences are so blatant that they smack you upside the head like Thor smiting Loki on the poster for an upcoming summer blockbuster. Other Viking hand-me-downs, like the Tooth Fairy or the song "London Bridge Is Falling Down," are a little less obvious. Viking culture and Norse mythology can be found front and center in everything from Led Zeppelin albums to *Final Fantasy* video games; from *Dungeons & Dragons* sessions to NASA space probes; from

The Lord of the Rings to popular cruise lines; and across all manner of television, movies, video games, comics, and books. They're everywhere you look, all portrayed at maximum volume and with varying degrees of historical accuracy. I mean, the Minnesota Vikings football team kicks off its pregame festivities by having a big bearded guy in a horned helmet charge onto the football field on a motorcycle screaming *"Vikiiiiiiiiiiings!"* while waving an enormous American flag.

But how many people outside Norway can even name one single Viking warrior? Who exactly were these guys, anyway?

Well, to be honest, it's not easy writing a history book about a bunch of mostly illiterate, bloodthirsty marauders who carved their stories into rocks more than a thousand years ago and credited their victories to blessings from hammer-swinging lightning gods. It's enough to make sane people crazy and historians even crazier.

Most of what we know about Vikings is brought to us by a cranky old thirteenth-century Icelandic lawyer/politician named Snorri Sturluson, who was pretty much the exact opposite of every Viking stereotype. Snorri was a brilliant legal mind and a devoted reader who constantly plotted and schemed to seize power in the government. He lost almost every battle he ever fought, fled the country twice, came back, and was eventually stabbed to death by three Vikings while cowering in his wine cellar. But even though this guy wasn't swinging axes and eating meat off the bone, he's probably the most important man in the study of Norse history because he's one of the only Norsemen who had the good sense to write everything down. And despite writing his material some three hundred years after the height of the Viking Age, he's also the best thing we have going for us these days as far as Viking history is concerned. Sure, some of the Christian monks who lived through the raids wrote things down, but it's hard to write something nice or useful about a group of guys who just burned your house to the ground and tried to kill you with an axe.

Some Viking sagas (old stories about Viking adventures) were passed down through the years as songs and poems, but things tend to get lost when you're playing a four-hundred-year-long game of telephone. Even though a lot of the sagas match up with legit sources from other parts of the world, there's also the occasional weird story where a hero makes pants out of sharks and has a ghost bear help him fight elves and fairies. This kind of thing seems less historically accurate.

Despite these problems, it's important to learn about these guys because they changed the entire course of human history in just a couple hundred years. Viking raiders would found Russia, become noblemen in France, sit as kings of England, and serve as bodyguards to mighty emperors. They'd build permanent settlements in France, Ireland, Iceland, and Holland and lay the foundations for cities such as

Dublin, York, and Reykjavík. They'd be the first Europeans to discover North America, trade goods along the Silk Road with China, and fight alongside Christian knights during the Crusades. And they'd do it all in the most awe-inspiring way imaginable—with gigantic bloodstained axes and cool boats that were shaped like dragons.

So we read the rocks with the stories carved into them. And we try to divine the truth from their songs and poems, to break out the facts from the legends. And we enjoy the ride along the way.

THE VIKING WARRIOR

The tactics, equipment, and ferocious might that terrorized the world for over two centuries

> Odin could make his enemies in battle blind, or deaf, or terror-struck, and their weapons so blunt that they could no more cut than a willow wand; on the other hand, his men rushed forwards without armor, were as mad as dogs or wolves, bit their shields, and were as strong as bears or wild bulls, and killed people at a blow, but neither fire nor iron told upon themselves. These were called Berserker.
>
> —Snorri Sturluson, Ynglinga Saga

FROM IRELAND TO RUSSIA, PARIS TO Constantinople, and everywhere in between, there was no more terrifying sight than a war band of gigantic Viking marauders clambering over the sides of their longships, crashing down into the ankle-deep surf, and charging forward with their armor shining in the sunlight, their axes and swords raised fearsomely above their heads. Although known by nearly a dozen different names—Northmen, Ashmen, Norsemen, Rus, Danes, Varangians, the Norse, and others—the people we now know as Vikings stood for hundreds of years as a symbol of ruin and destruction throughout the period of European history known as the Dark Ages. They were an unstoppable force that struck paralyzing fear into the hearts of all, from the lowliest peasants to the most heavily armored knights.

Vikings typically weren't professional warriors and raiders. Ravaging thatched-roof cottages with torches and steel was just something they did as a fun hobby and a way to make some extra cash in the summer. Family men, brothers, fathers, and sons, the Vikings came from all walks of life across Scandinavia—the regions of present-day Norway, Sweden, and Denmark. They embarked on their raiding expeditions for a variety of reasons ranging from glory, adventure, and wealth to the basic boring necessity of putting food on their tables during the long, cold Arctic winters. The only requirement was that each warrior had to provide his own gear.

In the early days of the Viking Age, the Northmen weren't organized into kingdoms and countries the way we think of them today. Their lands were really just a mishmash of minor dominions, each ruled by a guy known as a jarl. The jarls were responsible for recruiting their own men from their lands and putting together their own raiding parties; they did whatever they felt like without having to report to anyone in particular.

A jarl (sometimes they called themselves kings) would have a small bodyguard of professional warriors known as a *hird*. A jarl's *hird* would be made up of *hersir*, minor nobles who served him. The *hersir* would have all the best gear, get the most plunder, and join the jarl on raids and adventures. Below the *hersir* were freemen—landowners, farmers, and crafts-men. The freemen could join on as Vikings if they wanted, but they were required to serve in the jarl's levies, meaning that if the jarl was attacked by a rival gang of Viking warriors (something that happened more frequently than you might think), the freemen had to grab their spears and shields and defend their homes. At the bottom of the pecking order were the thralls—the slaves. Thralls had no rights and could be killed or sacrificed at their master's command, but if they had a good master, there was a chance he'd eventually let them buy or win their freedom. In a pinch, a thrall could be given a weapon and allowed to fight, but most Vikings didn't trust them enough to let that happen.

Although Viking gear varied wildly depending on how much the warrior was willing to spend on it, the typical

Norseman's primary weapon was a spear. He would carry two—a light javelin for throwing and a heavy spear for stabbing. The javelin had a barbed tip so it would stick into enemy shields, rendering them useless, and it was made of light-weight steel that would bend when it hit something, which prevented the enemy from throwing the warrior's javelin back at him. The heavy spear was made of ash wood, stood six to eight feet tall, and could be wielded in one hand, leaving the other hand free to hold a shield.

There were also two types of axes—the short axe, which was the perfect size for hiding behind the shield, and the much-feared Danish long axe: a six-foot-long, two-handed battle-axe with a single twelve-inch blade. It could cut through armor, horses, and men alike with one swing, shredding shields and splitting helmets like a chain saw through warm butter. The only downside to this weapon was that a warrior couldn't carry a shield with it, but the axe made up for it with sheer firepower. On more than one occasion, the Norse sagas refer to Vikings cutting through two and even three enemies with a single swing of the weapon.

Swords were an extraordinarily expensive item carried only by the richest Vikings, and were by far the most treasured weapon in the Viking arsenal. Given cool names like Gold-Hilt, Leg-Biter, and Long-and-Sharp, these double-edged straight blades were forged of iron, and their hilts were decorated in gold and silver and souped up with protective runes, healing stones, or bone fragments from animals or long-dead heroes. The legendary sword Skofnung, carried by King Hrolf Kraki, was said to be imbued with the spirits of twelve great heroes and would allegedly "sing" when it made contact with the enemy. (I picture this "song" sounding a lot like a guy yelling because he'd just been hit with a sword.)

A long, single-bladed knife called a sax rounded out the Viking arsenal, and it could be used for everything from shanking peasants to eating dinner. Some Vikings also carried bows, but even though all Norsemen could shoot well enough to hunt, they considered arrows a "coward's weapon" and far preferred to throw spears and rocks at their enemies or kill them face-to-face the old-fashioned way. (It's worth mentioning, however, that the Norse did have great respect for the Finns, who could ski downhill and accurately shoot arrows at the same time. Let's face it—that's cool.)

To defend themselves from their enemies, the Vikings wore armor fashioned from leather, bone, quilted fabric, or animal hide, and a helmet typically of the same material. *Hersir* warriors could sometimes afford imposing chain mail shirts that weighed in at about twenty-six pounds, as well as those cool-looking metal helmets with the eye and nose protection. But no matter how hard TV might try to convince you, real

Viking helmets didn't have horns on them. That touch was actually added by German opera costumers in the nineteenth century and is totally not legit. You seriously can't pick up a book about the Vikings without reading in the first twenty pages that there were no horned helmets. (Oh, sweet, it only took me fourteen.)

Finally, Vikings carried a brightly painted round shield made of wood, with a sturdy metal disk in the center to protect their hands. The shields were light and easy to carry and could be worn like a backpack by putting your arms through the leather strips on the back. But they wouldn't survive more than a few battles before needing to be replaced.

One group of guys who needed to replace their shields more often than everyone else was the terrifying *berserkir*, a group we know in English as the berserkers. Taking their name from the Norse word for "bear shirts," berserkers were a small, elite group of vicious, unruly warriors who went into battle completely naked except for a he-man-style loincloth and the pelt of either a wolf or a bear worn over their shoulders like a superhero's cape. These terrifying fighters howled and growled like animals and got so pumped up before battles that they would bite big chunks out of their shields before they attacked. Part of a mysterious cult dedicated to the god Odin, berserkers would prepare for battle the night before, sitting around a campfire drinking mysterious mushroom-based concoctions and working themselves up into a Super Mario rabid battle frenzy. Believing themselves to be possessed by Odin and the spirits of the animals whose pelts they wore, by the time battle began the next day, the berserkers would be frothing at the mouth like madmen, utterly freaking out anyone who saw them. They would always be the first to charge into battle, with such ferocity that today the phrase "going berserk" comes from these guys. They were almost completely immune to physical pain of any kind, and occasionally they could be found in intense hand-to-hand combat with trees, rocks, and other inanimate objects hours after the actual battle had ended.

Well, that's something, but most semi-sane Vikings

didn't actually want to encounter the enemy on the field of battle. These guys much preferred smash-and-grab plundering and raiding to out-and-out combat. There was a much smaller chance of being impaled when you were fighting disorganized peasants with pitchforks and rakes than when you were facing heavily armored royal cavalry who were packing lances and shields. When big-time, organized military battles did break out, the Vikings weren't just a horde of undisciplined wild men—they locked themselves into battle formation using a tactic known as the shield wall. A fairly common strategy in medieval times, the shield wall was basically a big line of guys who would interlock their shields, run at the enemy, and then stab with their spears to break the enemy's formation. Once the enemy line was broken, a second line of Viking axemen and swordmen would rush into the gap and start swinging for the fences. In large-scale battles, the Vikings lost about as many as they won—which is probably why they tried to avoid them.

Women did accompany the Vikings on their raids, but despite a few stories of hardcore warrior women known as shield-maidens raiding and fighting on the high seas, they mostly served as cooks, nurses, and healers. In addition to treating all the weird diseases that were pervasive throughout the Middle Ages (like leprosy, tuberculosis, and malaria),

women would patch up wounds, treat infections, repair broken gear, and diagnose everything from blood poisoning to tetanus. They would reset broken bones, amputate limbs when necessary, cut out arrowheads, and cauterize and sew up badly bleeding injuries, first salting the wound to numb it, then sealing it by touching it with a red-hot poker, and finally stitching it up with thread. Sometimes a woman would be both cook and surgeon. A typical after-battle feast was a gross-tasting soup made up of little more than onions and garlic. The next morning, the women would smell the stomachs of men who had been stabbed in the torso—if they could smell the garlic, it meant the man's stomach had been cut open, and nothing could be done to save him. He'd simply be left behind to die.

But that's the life of a Viking warrior for you. For many, all that awaited was a cruel, unceremonious, painful death alone in a hostile foreign land. But for those who made it through the dangers of Viking life, the promise of untold wealth and glory awaited. Poets were ready to sing the battle deeds of brave warriors and come up with epic nicknames for them to be remembered by. Gold and silver were sitting there for the taking from the wealthiest lands in Europe, and massive fame and fortune awaited all those who sought glory over long life.

WARRIORS AND...POETS?

Viking deeds of heroic greatness were recounted by Norse warrior-poets known as skalds, many of whom were just as efficient with a pen as they were with a broadsword. Known for its flowery depictions of incredibly brutal events, skaldic verse uses idioms, metaphors, and phrases called kenning that add a whole other layer of awesomeness to the writing. For instance, instead of saying "blood," a skald might say "corpse beer," "dew of slaughter," or "battle sweat." Death becomes "the sword's sleep." Ships are "sea-steeds," and battle is "the sword quarrel" or "weapon storm." Some of it makes sense, and some of it—like "Northern kiss" for a cold wind, or "ship of night" for the moon—can be really confusing. But how can you not like literature that reads like lyrics on a heavy metal album and changes "The king's men won the battle" to something like "The ring giver's children of battle weathered the weapon storm"? The guitar riff writes itself.

WHAT'S IN A NAME?

Tons of great Viking nicknames pop up throughout the sagas. Among my personal favorites are Haldar the Unchristian, Thord Horse-Head, Thorfinn Skull-Cleaver, Thorleif Goti the

Overbearing, Hrolf the Woman-Loving, Odd the Wide-Traveling, Sven Reaper, Harald Wartooth, Hadd the Hard, Olaf the Peacock, Erik the Priest-Hater, Einar Jingle-Scale, and Eyvind the Plagiarist. Most of these were proud nicknames for brave fighters, but this wasn't always the case—one Viking raider was mockingly nicknamed "the Children's Man," as a way of making fun of him because he once stopped another Viking from knocking over a baby's crib.

ULFBEHRT STEEL

The quality of Viking-era blades varied greatly, but the best by far was Ulfbehrt steel. Forged at a mysterious smithy in Frankland (present-day France and Germany), Ulfbehrt blades were wildly expensive and were carried only by the elite of the Viking world. Ulfbehrts were made with crucible steel, an incredibly pure steel that would not be produced in Europe until the 1700s, almost a thousand years later. Nobody knows who Ulfbehrt was or where he got his steel (some theorize he imported it from the Middle East through the Volga trade route with Russia), but his blades were flexible, wouldn't break in battle, kept their edge, and punched through any armor the Middle Ages had to offer. Ulfbehrt steel was so highly regarded that lesser smithies actually started producing cheap knockoffs to make a quick buck.

THE PREQUEL

Even though Lindisfarne, a small island off the northeast coast of England, is listed as the site of the first great Viking raid in Britain and the official beginning of the Viking Age, the first Viking longships actually appeared off the coast four years earlier. In 789, three ships rolled into the harbor of Portland, on the southwest coast of England, sailing up to the dock to check things out. The English harbormaster headed down to collect their docking fee, but the Vikings killed him with a spear, pushed off, and got out of there without paying their parking ticket. Some historians like to say this was the first real Viking raid in Europe, but it hardly counts.

THE WORLD in AD 800

One of the biggest pains in the butt about Viking history is that a lot of the places and peoples the Vikings ran into don't really exist anymore. For instance, modern-day England was actually four different countries in 800, and France and Germany were squished together into one big kingdom. China was still China, but almost the entire Middle East was ruled by one guy, Russia was made up of a hundred different little tribes, and nobody had even heard of North America because a lot of Europeans thought if you sailed west from Spain, you'd fall off the end of the earth and be eaten by a sea monster. It's annoying.

Well, to help out, here's a primer on some of the names and places that might have appeared on the map if a Viking war leader could have pulled up a GPS on his cell phone.

Tang Dynasty China

At this time, Eastern Asia was completely dominated by the unstoppable might of China. Led by the far-reaching emperors of the Tang Dynasty, China was the richest kingdom on earth and was in the middle of a golden age of learning, art, and music. Buddhist monks were worshipping in towering pagodas and monasteries; caravans loaded with gold, silks, and exotic goods were making their way up and down the famous Silk Road, which connected China to the Middle East; and Chinese scientists were inventing things like playing cards, government bureaucracy, and gunpowder, which they used mostly for fireworks and hand-held flamethrowers. Sure, the emperor Xuanzong had a few rebellions and barbarian uprisings to deal with, but that's par for the course when you're talking about imperial China.

Over in Korea, the kingdom of Silla was enjoying a cultural and economic happy fun time of its own, and in Southeast Asia the Khmer Empire was beginning to think about construction of an amazing, sprawling stone temple complex known as Angkor Wat. Just off the coast, Japan was entering the Nara period. A powerful emperor had recently moved the capital to Kyoto, and scholars were using the newly adopted Chinese system of writing to create impressive works of literature and poetry.

The Maya

The Americas hadn't been discovered yet, but that didn't mean there weren't people living there and doing cool things. The really big deal in the New World in the 800s was the Mayan Empire (located in present-day Mexico and Guatemala), which was building towering, pyramid-like limestone structures, making incredible advances in astronomy and mathematics, decorating its cities with the bleached skulls of its defeated enemies, and playing that cool-looking basketball game where the hoop is turned sideways and you can only hit the ball with your elbows or knees.

The Byzantine Empire

All of eastern Europe was controlled by the Byzantine Empire, a Roman dynasty run by a Greek emperor who lived in what is now the biggest city in Turkey. Confused yet?

Around AD 330, the once-powerful Roman Empire split in half, fracturing into the Western Roman Empire, based in Rome, and the Eastern Roman Empire, based in the incredibly wealthy fortress city of Constantinople, in what used to be Greece. The Western Empire was over-run by barbarians in 410 and completely fell apart, but Constantinople managed to fight off hordes of barbarian attackers from every direction and eventually grew into the richest and most dominant empire in Europe. Sitting on a golden throne behind the impenetrable triple walls of his mighty city, the Byzantine emperor ruled over millions of subjects and commanded absolute obedience from a mighty army that included everything from mercenary barbarian warriors to battle-hardened Greek armored troops.

The Abbasid Caliphate

The Islamic world was ruled by a guy known as the caliph, who was like a king, only he had a lot of religious power as well. His realm, known as the caliphate, was based in Baghdad, Iraq, and at this time dominated a huge swath of land stretching from the borders of the Byzantine Empire all the way through the Middle East and down across North Africa. The Abbasid caliph had just taken control of the

Muslim world from a rival dynasty known as the Umayyads in a bloody coup a few years earlier. (The Umayyads still held a stronghold in Spain, which bugged the Abbasids, but they couldn't really do anything about it.) All across the Muslim world a golden age was blossoming, with huge steps taken in architecture, mathematics, medicine, literature, and science. Muslim scholars and scientists built breathtaking mosques, ornate libraries, and astronomy observatories. Muslim universities began mass-producing paper for the first time, created calculus, and even invented the number zero, which I guess wasn't around until this point.

The British Isles

England, by comparison, was still basically in the Dark Ages. Far from being one unified Great Britain, England was divided up into four rival kingdoms (Northumbria, East Anglia, Wessex, and Mercia), each with some little king involved in his own annoying infighting against the other three. Ireland and Scotland were loose groups of Gaelic and Celtic clans without any overarching direction or central power structure, which made them easy targets for Viking marauders.

The Frankish Kingdom

On mainland Europe, the Vikings faced a hardcore enemy in 800. The lands of present-day France, Germany, Belgium, Switzerland, and the Netherlands were known

as the Frankish Kingdom and were ruled by the mighty
emperor Charlemagne—a big, scary German warrior-king
who had forged a Christian empire by marching on the barbarian tribes of Europe and unifying them, mostly by killing anyone who refused to be baptized Catholic. With the
backing of the pope in Rome, Charlemagne solidified his
rule with an iron fist, creating one of the most powerful
empires mainland Europe had ever seen.

Charlemagne had his first encounter with the Northmen
in the year 799, when a small band of Viking sea-raiders
attacked a settlement on the northern coast of present-day
France. The ruler of the Franks didn't hesitate to move
on this threat. He was a man of action, and he immediately ordered that huge fleets of warships be positioned at
the entrances of every major trade river that bordered the
North Sea. Vikings attempted a few small raids on his territory but were quickly turned away by stalwart lines of
imperial warships and fire-tipped arrows. The Danes never
gained a foothold in Charlemagne's domain as long as he
lived, but when he died in 814, he passed his empire to his
son Louis the Pious, who ultimately made a terrible mis-
take and divided the Frankish Empire into three smaller
kingdoms, giving one to each of his sons. Louis had hoped
this would keep his sons from killing one another in wars
of succession that would break his hard-won empire apart.
It didn't work.

The sons of Louis the Pious went to war immediately,

each trying to destroy the others and reunite Charlemagne's empire for themselves. They took all the fleets, warships, gold, and soldiers amassed through decades of prosperity and turned them on one another in a petty blood feud for power.

The road was now open for the Vikings to do their thing. They attacked without mercy. The once-prosperous port city of Dorestad was sacked four times in four years, from 834 to 837. The former capital at Rouen was laid waste. The Rhine, Loire, and Seine Rivers were plundered ruthlessly, with Vikings killing bishops, burning towns, grabbing slaves, looting, destroying, and leaving nothing but smoldering embers in their wake. In 845, a Viking called Ragnar Hairy-Breeches defeated an imperial force and sacked Paris, stripping the outer ring of the city of its valuables before accepting payment of seven thousand pounds of silver to leave. Flanders, the Rhineland, and Picardy, almost completely undefended, were ravaged. Charles the Bald, one of Louis's sons and now emperor of the Western Frankish Kingdom (basically modern-day France), was so caught up in his own petty arguments that he did nothing, offering payments to Viking leaders in 858, 863, 866, and 867 just to leave him alone. Little did he know this was only the beginning of what the Vikings would have in store.

KNOW YOUR VIKINGS

NAME:
Harald "Wartooth" Hraereksson

RANK:
King of Zealand,
a heavily populated island in Denmark

RELIGION:
Pagan

BORN:
Denmark, probably late 600s

DIED:
Killed in the Battle of Bravalla around 750

AREAS OF OPERATION:
Denmark, Norway

NOTEWORTHY:
Semi-legendary Danish war leader sometimes
referred to as the "First Viking"; was allegedly
150 years old at the time of his death

NORSE MYTHOLOGY

Ragnarok and other optimistic outlooks on life

> That one is called Surt, who sits there at the end of the world as a guardian. He has a burning sword, and at the end of the world he will travel and harry and defeat all the gods and burn the entire world with fire.

—Snorri Sturluson, *Gylfaginning*

DO YOU LIKE DWARVES, ELVES, AND FROST giants? Those are all mythical creatures that served as part of the Norse religion. So are fairies, trolls, and mermaids. Entire *Pokémon* worlds have been built around

Viking concepts, and Norse mythology is heavily featured in games like *Skyrim*, the *Final Fantasy* series, and all things *Dungeons & Dragons*. Does your little sister like the Disney movie *Frozen*? It's based on a story called "The Snow Queen," which was written by Danish author Hans Christian Andersen. He drew a lot of his fairy-tale ideas from Norse mythology and also wrote "The Little Mermaid." If ice or water isn't your thing, the concept of Hell as an underworld full of dead people and fire is also drawn from Norse religion. So is Santa Claus.

Intrigued yet? Think of it this way: The word *Thursday* comes from "Thor's Day," meaning that you literally can't go a week without having to deal with something involving Norse mythology.

Besides being the basis for many things that are awesome, Norse myth is also a really good way to understand what was going on in the mind of the average Viking during the 800s. The Vikings' religion was brutal, bloody, violent, and based on sacrifice, death, war, and glory in battle—all concepts that the Vikings took to heart and that made them incredibly powerful, fearless, and deadly on a battlefield.

Norse mythology starts with the universe being one huge, empty space of nothingness populated by just a couple of random gods. One day, an enormous frost giant named Ymir popped up out of nowhere, along with his giant Babe the

Blue Ox–style pet space cow. Ymir started spawning a race of frost giants—nine-foot-tall bearded guys with bad attitudes— which bothered the gods, because they felt like they should be the only people allowed to make new things happen in the universe. The gods got mad and killed Ymir by pulling him apart with their bare hands and turning his head into the sky, his body into the earth, and his blood into the oceans. So every time you jump in the ocean, you're swimming in giant blood. Which is gross. The sagas don't mention what happened to the cow, but my money is on "epic cosmic beef jerky."

The Vikings' entire concept of reality is based on something called the World Tree. Basically, there's a big tree. Right in the dead center of it is a flat plane of existence known as Middle Earth (yes, you read that correctly). This place is home to humans, but also to light elves, dark elves, dwarves, fairies, pixies, giants, and other nonreal fairy-tale things. The earth is the earth, but if you sail too far out into the ocean, you'll run into the Midgard Serpent, which is a humongous snakelike sea monster that encircles the entire world and has a bite so venomous that it can even kill gods. Keep this concept in mind when you read in chapter 18 about Leif Eriksson sailing out into uncharted waters on his way to discover the New World.

Vikings believed that rainbows were actually highways

to Heaven, and that if you were somehow able to defy the laws of physics and ride your horse up a rainbow, you'd end up in Viking Heaven at the top of the World Tree. This realm is called Asgard, and it's home to all the gods and their huge golden palaces. If you go the other direction on the rainbow and drop down below the ground, you end up in Hel, which is a nightmarish realm run by a demonic goddess also named Hel. She looks kind of like the Batman villain Two-Face because half of her body is pale white and the other is pitch-black. Her home features a waist-deep river of blood, big snakes that spit poison in people's eyes, and a huge, scary dragon named Nidhogg that spends its time snacking on dead bodies. As an excellent side note, there is a big eagle sitting at the top of the World Tree, and a little squirrel named Drill-Tooth spends all day running back and forth to pass insults between the eagle and Nidhogg the dragon.

At the center of Asgard, in the golden walls of his magical palace, Valhalla, sits the king of the gods—Odin the All-Father. Odin is the god of death and war, magic and wisdom. He's a complicated guy who not only inspires Viking berserkers to tear their enemies limb from limb, but also provides artistic and spiritual inspiration to prose writers, poets, and mystics. Odin flies around Asgard on a super-fast eight-legged horse named Sleipnir, casts spells, and has a spear called Gungnir that never misses when thrown at his enemies. Odin has only one eye, but he can see the future, which is so frightening to him that it makes him depressed. He also invented the Vikings' written language by impaling himself on the World Tree with his own spear and thinking a lot while he hung there for nine days straight.

Once a year, during the Yule Festival for the winter solstice, Odin dresses up in a bloodred suit and makes himself berserk, and he and Sleipnir fly through the night sky along with an army of ghost Vikings and ravens. Anyone unlucky enough to witness this flight, known as the Wild Hunt, would die of fright on the spot. In later years, after the Norse stopped worshipping Odin and became Christians, they changed this myth around a little bit. The eight-legged horse became eight reindeer, Odin mixed with the Christian saint Nicholas to become Santa Claus, and "instant death" became "hooray for Christmas presents."

Odin's palace, Valhalla, is the final resting place for great Viking warriors who have died gloriously in battle. If you were a Norseman, this was where you wanted to be. After a big fight, Odin would send his assistants—a host of angelic, heavily armored warrior-maidens known as Valkyries, who zoom around the battlefield on flying horses—to collect the souls of the greatest fighters among the dead. The Valkyries

bring the souls back to Valhalla, where the ghost Vikings spend their eternity training for a huge battle between good and evil that will take place at the end of the world.

The routine for a ghost warrior in Odin's hall goes like this: You wake up in the morning, put on all your battle gear, and go out into a huge field, where every warrior in Valhalla has an insane fight to the death. At the end of the day, after almost everyone has been killed and their body parts are strewn across the battlefield, you all get magically resurrected and return to Valhalla to talk about the battle, drink tons of mead and ale, eat unlimited bacon and pork, sing war chants, and fall asleep. Then you wake up in the morning and do it all over again. It's sort of like sleepaway baseball camp, but with battle-axes, and you're allowed to repeatedly kill the people you don't like.

While Odin is the ruler of the Norse gods, his son Thor, the god of lightning, thunder, storms, and the ocean, is by far the most popular. His primary job in Asgard is to kill giants by smashing them to bits with a gigantic magical hammer called Mjolnir. A warrior of unmatched strength and an expert at hand-to-hand combat, Thor can also throw Mjolnir at giants with perfect accuracy, and his weapon returns to his hand immediately after conking a giant in the face. Thor is so hardcore that Vikings believed thunder was the sound of Thor clubbing a frost giant unconscious up in Heaven.

A great hero, a mighty warrior, and a destroyer of all

things evil or weak, Thor was the god you wanted to call on right before you charged into battle with the enemy. Most Vikings also prayed to him for protection before they set sail on the ocean or headed out on raids, because Thor was the god of crossing waterways. It was common for Viking men and women to wear necklaces featuring small metal depictions of Thor's hammer.

When he's not smashing giants by drilling them in the head with Mjolnir, Thor also loves to drink mead, an alcoholic beverage made from fermented honey. According to Norse myth, the tides of the ocean were created when a giant turned the ocean into mead and challenged Thor to a drinking contest. Thor chugged so much of it that he set it sloshing around.

Another important celestial being is Freya, the Norse goddess of love, fertility, beauty, and war—and it should say something about the Vikings' society that their goddess of love is also the goddess of war. Wearing a cloak of falcon feathers and crying tears of gold for the men who died in combat, Freya is the leader of the Valkyries and the most beautiful of the goddesses. She determines who will have babies, who will fall in love with whom, and who will die gloriously in battle. After a battle is over, she takes all the dead Odin leaves behind and brings them to her palace, called Sessrúmnir. Nobody really knows what happens in Sessrúmnir, though, because anything that was written about it doesn't exist anymore. It was probably pretty fun, though.

The other guy you should know about is the diabolical trickster god Loki—a jokester who plays a lot of mean pranks on the gods but eventually spirals into darkness and becomes known as "the Slanderer of the Gods and the Disgrace of All Gods and Men." Loki is the son of Odin and a frost giant woman, and his children include the goddess Hel and the giant, venomous Midgard Serpent.

In the first part of the mythology, Loki is shown as a happy-go-lucky guy who can shape-shift into different animals and loves pulling practical jokes on the gods. He hides Freya's locket, tricks Thor into dressing up like a woman and getting into a fight without his magic hammer, and drinks Odin's milk right out of the carton when he's not paying attention. Everyone kind of laughs off Loki's jokes and treats him like an annoying little brother. But they don't have much of a sense of humor when Loki murders the god Baldur by tricking a blind guy into throwing mistletoe at him during a party. (Don't ask me how Baldur dies from having a sprig of mistletoe thrown at him....It doesn't make any sense to me, either.)

Well, Baldur is another son of Odin, and he's the god of light, happiness, and being cool to people, so when Loki has him whacked, everyone gets super, *super* mad about it. Thor tracks Loki down, corners him in a river, and beats him in a fight. Loki tries to turn into a salmon and swim away, but Thor grabs him by the fish tail and hauls him down to the underworld, where Odin ties Loki to a big rock. Loki now struggles against this rock day and night, and the Vikings believed that earthquakes were caused by the cranky tied-up god screaming out in anger and trying to break free. Loki is joined down in Hel by Nidhogg the dragon, a bunch of monsters, and the ghostly souls of murderers, cheaters, liars, and men who had the nerve to die of boring things like old age and illness and not be killed in battle like all good Vikings should.

Remember that I said Odin is depressed because he can see the future? Well, in Norse mythology, the future is really dark and messed up. The story goes that Loki will one day break free from his nightmarish prison and lead all the monsters and souls of Hel in a huge, epic, earth-shattering war against Odin, the gods, and the spirits of those ghost Vikings who have been training in Valhalla.

The battle is known as Ragnarok, meaning "the Twilight of the Gods."

It starts with Fimbulvetr, "the Great Winter," when three years of snow turn the earth into a huge ball of ice. The sun burns out and throws the world into eternal night. A big wolf called the Moon Dog takes a bite out of the moon, which splatters the earth, sky, and heavens with blood. Loki comes up from the ground with the souls of the dead and a horde of skyscraper-sized carnivorous monsters. The frost giants arrive aboard *Naglfar*, the Death Ship, an enormous, gross vessel created from the fingernails of the dead. Odin, Freya, Thor, and the Vikings of Valhalla and Sessrúmnir ride down the Rainbow Bridge, armed to the teeth, dressed in their strongest golden armor, and ready for anything.

The two armies smash together in a battle so intense that

it destroys the known universe. Odin is eaten by the giant wolf Fenris, so his son Vidar, the god of vengeance, goes into a blood rage and rips Fenris in half with his bare hands. Garm, an evil version of Clifford the Big Red Dog, kills the war god Tyr, then dies from a mortal wound. Loki and the god Heimdall stab each other to death at the exact same time. The Midgard Serpent is dropped by a mighty blow from Thor's hammer, but not before it bites Thor, and the god of thunder falls dead from poison moments after defeating his foe. Surrounded by dying monsters and gods, the leader of the giants, a Godzilla-sized Viking named Surt, swings a flaming two-handed sword the size of the Empire State Building and sets the entire World Tree on fire.

Once the raging inferno of superheated flame finally dies down, there are only six creatures left standing—two sons of Odin, two sons of Thor, and a human man and woman. The two humans will eventually repopulate the earth, and a new age of peace will take over and reign for the rest of eternity. Which is a semi-nice silver lining in a brutally dark religion.

For better or worse, this is what the early pagan Vikings believed—that each warrior was living this life as training so that he could hopefully die gloriously in battle, be taken to Valhalla, and spend eternity preparing to destroy the universe in an earth-shattering war between demons and gods.

These are definitely not the sort of people you want to have coming after you on a battlefield.

ϟ   ϟ   ϟ

DAYS OF THE WEEK

Four days of the week are named for Norse gods: Tuesday is "Tyr's Day" (named for the Norse god of battle), Wednesday is "Odin's Day" (in some cultures, *Odin* is spelled *Woden*), Thursday is "Thor's Day," and Friday is "Freya's Day." In case you were curious, Sunday is "the Sun's Day," Monday is "the Moon's Day," and Saturday is named for Saturn, the Roman god of time.

WALKING INTO MORDOR

If a lot of this elves, dwarves, and giants stuff sounds familiar, it's because J. R. R. Tolkien was a professor of the Anglo-Saxon language (the Germanic language spoken by the people of England before it evolved into English as we know it today), was fluent in Old Norse, and had read all the Viking mythological texts in their original language. Many of the names in his *Lord of the Rings*—like Gandalf, Sauron, and Middle-earth—were taken directly from Norse texts.

THE VALHALLA FUNERAL

After death, some Viking chieftains were cremated alongside all their favorite possessions in a ceremony that was believed to take them directly to Valhalla. The chief would be dressed in his nicest clothes (don't want to look like a schlub for Odin) and placed in a tent on his ship, and then his servants would bring everything from horses to still-breathing slave girls to join him on his vessel. Once everything was in place, the chief's sons and *hersir* would light the entire thing on fire. After the fire died down, the Vikings would heap dirt on top of the ashes, build a burial mound, and then mark the place with a really nice statue or tombstone.

COVERING THEIR BASES

Later in their history, the Norsemen began to adopt Christianity, yet many of these devoted new Viking Christians still held on to their love of the ancient ways just to keep their bases covered. For instance, a salty old Norse sailor once remarked that when the seas were calm he prayed to Jesus Christ, but when the seas were rough he prayed to Thor. There are plenty of archaeological examples of Thor's hammer necklaces that also have a tiny cross (a symbol of Christianity) carved into the center.

KNOW YOUR
VIKING HISTORY

NAME:
Thor, son of Odin

RANK:
Norse god of thunder

RELIGION:
Himself

BORN:
Beginning of recorded time

DIED:
Will be killed by a giant serpent in the great battle
of Ragnarok at the end of recorded time

AREAS OF OPERATION:
Asgard, Midgard, Giant Land, the ocean

NOTEWORTHY:
Can kill most frost giants with a single swing of his hammer,
hitting them so hard it creates thunder and lightning

TURGEIS THE DEVIL

The Butcher of Clonmacnoise
AD 839–845

> To attempt to follow, through all its frightful details, the course of outrage and massacre which continued to be pursued by the bands of Turgesius throughout the remainder of that tyrant's turbulent life would be a task as wearisome as it is revolting.

—Thomas Moore, *The History of Ireland*

EVERY SO OFTEN IN HUMAN HISTORY, A GUY comes along who is so impossibly cruel and utterly unredeemable that the only logical conclusion is that he is the physical embodiment of pure evil packed into human form.

In ninth-century Ireland, that man was a faceless cata-
clysm of destruction known throughout history as Turgeis
the Devil: the Butcher of Clonmacnoise, the founder of Dublin,
and, to this day, one of the most hated men in the history of
the Emerald Isle.

When Turgeis (also called Turgesius) the Devil swept
into Ireland, it wasn't the first time the Irish had encountered Vikings; the Norse had been making their trademark
ultra-violent raids on the shores of the island since the late
790s. By the time Turgeis and his men showed up for the
pillage party in 839, the hapless fishing villages of Ireland
had already suffered through roughly forty years of intermit-
tent (and totally annoying) pillaging and rampaging at the
hands of angry Scandinavians in wolf pelts. It didn't really
shake them up all that much anymore.

What truly set Turgeis apart was that this guy took a
well-established formula and cranked it into overdrive—not
just in sheer scale but also in brutality.

Like many Vikings, Turgeis realized that storming
through a village, setting fire to thatched-roof cottages, and
kicking peasants with a boot made of reindeer fur was fun,
but your typical fisherman and dirt farmer weren't exactly
dripping with gold and jewels and microwave ovens or other
fabulous prizes. This powerful, coordinated, motivated Viking
ruler realized instead that the key to success was to single out
ultra-holy religious sites like churches, abbeys, convents, and

monasteries—because, for some reason, Catholics really liked to stock their places of worship full of golden treasures, and the only people guarding them were a bunch of unarmed holy men equipped with little more than burlap sacks, leather-bound manuscripts, and a vow of nonviolence. For an illiterate, Odin-worshipping conqueror like Turgeis, who wouldn't know the difference between a crucifix and a Big Mac if it was handed to him by the Hamburglar, the solution here was easy: Attack

churches. It provides all the excitement of killing, maiming, and destroying, plus it hits your enemy where it hurts, and you can make a little cash in the process.

So in 839, Turgeis started big. He arrived with the most obscenely humongous Viking fleet Ireland had ever seen, and went straight for the crown jewel of Christianity in one of the most devoutly Christian places in the world. The Devil launched an attack on the city of Armagh—which at the time was the single holiest place in Ireland, the seat of the Catholic Church on the island, and the home of the venerated saint Patrick's remains. (Yes, we are talking about *that* Saint Patrick, the dude with the green cupcakes and the snakes and all that.) After three full-scale assaults against a fanatically determined but badly outnumbered force of dedicated Irish peasant warriors—none of whom were expecting to be attacked by Vikings in the middle of the night—the torch-bearing Norsemen battled their way over the walls of Armagh and looted without care. While one brave Irish abbot did manage to escape with the shrine of Saint Patrick, the Vikings went nuts on everything else, killing monks and students, knocking over altars, and making the whole "Oops, now you're getting pinched by everyone in the class because you forgot to wear green on Saint Patrick's Day" thing look like a fun afternoon at a water park. According to some admittedly biased but understandably enraged Irish chroniclers, Turgeis's wife, Ota (a priestess of Odin), even dared to

offer up animal sacrifices in the chapel (something that most ninth-century Catholic monks would consider pretty heinous).

A year later, after Armagh was mostly rebuilt, Turgeis came back and sacked it again, just to be a jerk. A couple of years after that, he did roughly the same thing to the second-holiest city in Ireland, sailing up the Shannon River with sixty ships and attacking the abbey at Clonmacnoise—a center of culture and learning that attracted students from as far away as England and France.

While this unprovoked attack on Ireland's holiest cities scandalized every single Catholic on the island and gave them all something just short of a heart attack, Turgeis the Devil was only getting started. For the next six years, the Viking warlord sent wave after wave of his longships as far inland as they could get, penetrating up the Boyne, Liffey, and Shannon Rivers and attacking towns that until this point had been utterly untouched by the Viking scourge. He sacked Meath, Clonfert, and Connacht, then hit Armagh a couple more times just for good measure.

And what's worse, not only did the Devil defile basically every church and holy place in Ireland that was accessible by river, but he also didn't have the good sense to slink away into the night when he was done. He stayed behind, drank all their whiskey, ate all their food, deposed the local governments (mostly by executing them), and then divided the land up among his own loyal soldiers who'd helped him conquer the joint. Before long, so much of central and western Ireland was under Viking control that Turgeis the Devil is actually listed among the kings of Ireland in some historical registers (with a notable one mentioning that he "ruled in peace" but that "the peace was a troubled one and its tranquility was often disturbed").

In addition to forging the first Viking state in Western Europe with the blade edge of his axe, Turgeis the Devil is also notable for founding the city of Dublin in 841. Turgeis saw this region, an area that had previously been known to the locals as Dubh-Linn ("the Black Pool"), as a good narrow spot across the Liffey River and decided to set up a trading settlement there to help ship his plundered goods back to Norway or Denmark or wherever the heck he was actually from. In the process, he ended up establishing the town that nowadays serves as the capital of Ireland.

Now, okay, fine, founding Dublin is cool and all, but it was still pretty obvious to every red-blooded Irishman that this dude absolutely had to die. There are a couple of different stories about how Turgeis the Devil met his inevitable fate. The one I prefer goes like this: The Irish king Máel Seachnaill eventually got sick of trying to rule a kingdom that shared a border with a new Viking kingdom, so he sent a message to Turgeis saying he would marry his daughter to Turgeis's son to forge an alliance between the two kingdoms. When Turgeis and his men reached the designated meeting place, they saw the princess and fifteen of her handmaidens standing there waiting for them. The Vikings ran over to them, but when they got up close, they were horrified to discover that instead of hot girls, the handmaidens were *dudes with knives*, who shanked the Vikings and captured Turgeis the Devil. Máel Seachnaill then had Turgeis beaten up and tortured before binding him in chains and drowning him in a lake known as Lough Owel.

Unlike some horror-movie villains in similar situations, Turgeis the Devil never resurfaced.

But the story of the Vikings in Ireland doesn't end with Turgeis the Devil. Interestingly, for the next 150 years or so, the Vikings trickled into Ireland through the Viking base at Dublin, and before long they'd begun to integrate themselves into Irish society. Over time, they married Irish women, gave their sons Celtic names, started becoming Christian, and even started wearing Irish-style clothing and jewelry. Rather than acting as conquerors and raiders (although there was plenty of that), the Vikings mainly set up Ireland as a trading center. The Emerald Isle had plenty of tradable resources but not really reliable sea travel, so Vikings established cities at Cork, Limerick, Wexford, and other places to ferry goods back and forth between Ireland and the rest of Europe. The more military-minded of the Viking warriors lent out their services to warring Irish clans as mercenaries, becoming

warriors-for-hire and kicking butts across Ireland for which-
ever Celtic king happened to be the highest bidder.

The Irish kings won a major victory against the Vikings
of Dublin in AD 980, but the event traditionally pegged as
the end of the Viking Age in Ireland is the Battle of Clontarf
in 1014. Here, the famous Irish king Brian Boru went up
against a large Viking force led by a hardcore Norseman
named Brodir of Man. During the battle, Brian Boru was
slain by Brodir, but his chief general—the Irish death-dealer
known to history only as Wolf the Quarrelsome—carried the
attack and destroyed the Viking forces. To avenge his king,
Wolf the Quarrelsome then executed Brodir of Man in a horribly diabolical manner that involved pulling out his insides,
ensuring that the Vikings would cease to exist as a political
power in Ireland.

mcVikings

When you're talking about Irish, Celtic, and Gaelic last names,
the prefixes *Mc* and *Mac* simply mean "son of." Years of inter-
mingling between those cultures and the Norsemen led to the
creation of many new "McViking" last names—for instance,
MacSweeney means "son of Svein," a traditional Nordic name.
Along the same lines, *MacLeod* means "son of Ljot," and *MacIver*
means "son of Ivar."

WARRIOR-KINGS

It was not unusual for the king himself, surrounded by his loyal bodyguards, to personally lead his Viking army onto the field to fight under a towering battle flag. One time, an eleventh-century Viking king, Magnus Barelegs of Norway (he was called "Barelegs" because he conquered Scotland, loved kilts, and decided to wear them all the time), was charging out at the head of his army in a chain mail shirt and a kilt. One of his assistants was like, "Don't you want to stay in the back and maybe wear some pants or something?" Magnus, a true warrior Viking lord, replied, "Kings are made for honor, not for long life."

THE VIKING AGE

While exact dates are pretty dicey, most historians agree that the Viking Age in Europe begins with the Viking attack on Lindisfarne Island in AD 793 and continues through the Norman Conquest of England in 1066. These 273 years are just a little blip on the radar of history, but try thinking about it this way: The Viking Age lasted about as long as the United States of America has been a country. That should put things in perspective.

THE VIKING
LONGSHIP

Without question, no invention was more important to the Viking way of life than the longship.

Created from thin, lightweight, flexible oak planks nailed together in an overlapping pattern, the longships were stronger, lighter, and more seaworthy than anything else in the world at the time. Waterproofed with seal blubber, oil, and pine tar, the longship was highly functional on open water and was equipped with a sturdy forty-foot mast boasting a large red-and-white square sail that the village's women stitched together from thin strips of hemp or wool. Rigged with rope made from hemp or horsehair, a ship could go seventeen to twenty-five miles per hour under sail. It also had several rows of oars in case the Vikings wanted to move it the old-fashioned way.

The great thing about the longship was that it was fast and versatile but could also hold up on long ocean voyages. For starters, it had a very shallow draft, meaning it could float, fully loaded with Vikings, in just three feet of water. This allowed the Vikings to go places that big, lumbering warships couldn't go, and their ability to attack undefended villages way inland on a tiny river helped give them the element of surprise. Plus the ship was shaped

like a canoe and could go in either direction equally well, so they could beach it, attack, load up the ship, push off, and sail right back the way they came without having to turn the boat around. It was also light enough that a couple of guys could pick up the entire boat and carry it if they had to.

The longship had something called a keel, which is a big surfboard-like fin-looking thing that goes underneath the entire ship and keeps it from flipping over in a nasty storm. The Vikings were the first people to use keels, meaning that their small longships actually worked in rough ocean storms just about as well as any ship in history up until this point.

The longship was navigated by the positions of the sun and stars, and aside from a weather vane on top of the mast, there were no instruments to speak of—the Vikings kind of had to wing it and hope they knew where they were going. The longship was steered with a ten-foot rudder, operated by a guy who stood at the back right-hand side of the ship. If you've ever wondered why the right side of a ship is called "starboard," it's from the Viking word *styrboard*, meaning "steering side," because that's where the rudder was.

The Vikings had two kinds of ships—the *knarr*, a trading ship, and the *drakkar*, or "dragon ship," which was a warship. The size of a *drakkar* varied, with a typical one being about seventy-six feet long, with sixteen oars to a side. Thirty or forty men could fit in a standard *drakkar*, but there were others that could hold over a hundred warriors. There was no "below deck" on this ship, so Vikings would sit on their sea chests, hang their shields on the railing of the ship (not just to look cool but also to protect themselves against enemy arrows fired from shore), and just row all day. With no shelter, they'd be stuck outside when it rained, be exposed to the elements sometimes for weeks at a time, and sleep on the deck in sleeping bags made from sealskin.

Knarr were about fifty feet long, with fewer crew, but they had a hold belowdecks where merchandise to be traded could be stored.

With names like *Long Serpent*, *Oar Steed*, and *Surf Dragon* (gnarly, dude), these warships were decorated with fierce dragon heads that were designed to inspire terror in their victims. It usually worked.

KNOW YOUR VIKINGS

NAME:
Turgeis "the Devil"

RANK:
King of Dublin

RELIGION:
Pagan

BORN:
Probably Norway, early 800s

DIED:
Executed by drowning
in Lough Owel, Ireland, 845

AREA OF OPERATION:
Ireland

NOTEWORTHY:
Founded the city of Dublin
and commanded dozens of successful and
devastating raids across Ireland

THE VOYAGE OF HASTING

A fearsome Viking warrior proves that no civilization is safe from the wrath of the Norsemen
AD 859–861

This accursed and headstrong, extremely cruel and harsh, destructive, troublesome, wild, ferocious, infamous... inconstant, brash, conceited and lawless, death-dealing, rude, suspicious, rebellious traitor and kindler of evil...through such accursed deeds is he more monstrous than the rest, that he ought not be marked by ink but by charcoal. He has defiled nations, flying hither and thither; he has claimed their wealth for himself and his followers.

—Dudo of Saint Quentin, cranky Frankish monk

I**N 859, A VIKING LEADER NAMED HASTING** launched the most epic, wide-ranging raiding voyage the Norsemen would ever undertake in their impressive careers: a three-year, full-scale attack by sixty-two longships that brought bloody, sword-swinging havoc and ever-burning torches to the doorsteps of Spanish kings, Muslim emirs, and Italian counts. The raiders pillaged North Africa, the southern part of France, and the coasts of Sicily. Smelting unsuspecting villages into charcoal all along the way, this intense Viking ruler may even have traveled as far as Egypt and Palestine, all before finally returning home with a haul of loot that made every man on the voyage an instant celebrity.

Hasting's raiders encountered thousands of hostile warriors of every shape and size. They plundered priceless artifacts from mosques, temples, and churches alike, and fearlessly stared down primitive ship-mounted flamethrowers—terrifying weapons that spewed out screaming-hot jets of burning fuel capable of lighting up Viking longboats like prematurely Valhalla-bound funeral pyres.

In the year 859, the already famous Danish warlord Hasting decided he was not content with simply plundering the Viking "greatest hits" in England and France. It was time to do something so incredibly over-the-top that everyone in history would remember him as the most baller Norseman to ever huck a throwing axe. So he teamed up with a similarly minded warrior, the excellently named Bjorn Ironside, and prepared for action. Bjorn was said to be the son of a dude named Ragnar Hairy-Breeches, a Viking warlord so incredible that most historians don't even believe he was a real guy. I'll talk more about Ragnar in chapter 7, but for right now the important thing to know about Bjorn is that he was so gigantic, tough, and terrifying in combat that a legend eventually arose claiming that when he was a baby, his mom dipped him in a vat of magical liquid that made him completely impervious to conventional weapons (this is probably not true).

It should be mentioned here that while it was fun to plunder the English and the Franks, the most powerful, advanced, and wealthiest kingdoms in the world in 850 were the Byzantine Empire in Greece and the Islamic caliphates of Spain and the Middle East. The Vikings typically didn't bother raiding these mighty empires, mostly because those guys had the money, resources, and intelligence to actually fight back effectively, and it was way too dangerous to attack them head-on. Most Vikings preferred to go for the easy pickings and were happy settling for smaller piles of treasure if it meant they weren't going to end up dead on a battlefield somewhere with a sword sticking out of them.

Bjorn Ironsides and Hasting weren't concerned with that. They were going for it.

It helped that Hasting was already in a weird spot with the Franks. He'd made quite a living out of pillaging up and down the Seine River for the past few years, but around 859 the Frankish king Charles the Bald gave Hasting a bunch of money and land to stop burning his towns and monasteries. Hasting took the money and land but didn't exactly trust the Frankish king not to stab him in the back the second he turned around. So he immediately sold the land to some wealthy French baron and used the money to buy sixty-two longships and hire a bunch of warriors for his raid on Spain.

This wouldn't be the first time Vikings tried to undertake an operation against Islamic Spain. Fifteen years earlier, a group of enterprising warriors had captured Lisbon (in present-day Portugal) and plundered the ultra-wealthy Muslim stronghold city of Seville, but it didn't work out too well for them. The Muslim emir, Abd al-Rahman II, counterattacked with a huge army while the Vikings were looting Seville. The emir smashed the Viking forces with catapults, heavy cavalry, and a screaming horde of scimitar-swinging warriors; burned their ships in port; and then sent the heads of two hundred Vikings to his friends in Tangiers just to prove to his buddies that, hey, maybe these Norse guys weren't all they were cracked up to be. The Norsemen who were lucky enough to survive had to leave all their treasure behind, and future jarls weren't exactly excited about the prospect of a repeat performance.

Of course, Hasting and Bjorn Ironside weren't your typical

Vikings, and it would take a lot more than a decapitation-happy
emir to derail these big, scary Norsemen from their target.
They attacked towns across the Iberian Peninsula and "did
many evil things in Spain, both destroying and plundering"
(according to one very unhappy monk) while raiding Christian
settlements in present-day Spain and Portugal. They were
apparently pretty successful, because when Muslim warships
captured two Viking longships that had been blown off course
in a storm, they found them packed full of gold, treasure, and
slaves.

Confident of his invincibility, Hasting and his sixty remaining ships continued heading along the coast, but thanks to
those two dudes getting blown off course, the caliphate had
already had a sneak peek at what was coming their way.
And by the time Hasting's fleet arrived in southern Spain,
the Muslims were ready for him. Hasting attempted a couple
of attacks but found the emir's defenses too strong to pene-
trate. Instead of turning back, however, he just went around
the coast of Spain, crossing through the Strait of Gibraltar
into the Mediterranean Sea, and started attacking the North
African villages and towns of a completely different caliphate.
The last thing those dudes living on the edge of the Sahara
Desert expected to see on a Tuesday morning was a fleet of
Viking warships sailing into the harbor full of six-foot-tall
Swedish and Norwegian guys carrying two-handed long axes.

The Vikings sacked Nekor in present-day Morocco, stripped the mosque of every ounce of gold and silver, killed the leaders, and captured hundreds of slaves. In Mauretania, they were attacked by an army of scimitar-swinging Moors (dark-skinned North African Muslims), but Viking warriors cut off the king's hand, drove his army from the field, and had their way with his capital. The one-handed king paid a ransom for the Norsemen to release a few of their more important prisoners, but Hasting kept the rest. A few years after this, Irish chroniclers and historians started remarking about a bunch of mysterious "black people" and "blue people" living in Dublin, usually as slaves.

After North Africa, Hasting and Bjorn Ironside hit the southern coast of Spain, attacked the Balearic Islands, then set up camp for the winter on Camargue, a deserted little island with a decent harbor just off the southern coast of France. They chilled there during the winter of 859, and as soon as the weather got nicer, they took a sweet little cruise up the Rhône River and along what would become the French Riviera, enjoying the sights, hanging out on the beaches, and burning the city of Valence to the ground.

While he was in the area, Hasting thought it might be kind of rad to pop in and see what he could gank from the most famous city in the world—Rome, Italy. Rome had fallen on hard times since the glory days of the Roman Empire three hundred years earlier, but the Eternal City was still a juicy target for pillagers and barbarians, and Hasting was convinced that if he could sack Rome, he would truly be remembered forever as the LeBron James of incinerating cities.

In 860, Hasting and Bjorn Ironside sailed toward Italy. Before long, they saw huge walls in the distance—a towering city, filled with riches. It was the most amazing place Hasting had ever seen. He knew this was it.

The defenses of the city were far too strong to overcome with a mere sixty ships, so Hasting developed a semi-hilariously diabolical plan to bluff his way into striking distance.

Hasting parked his fleet in the harbor, then sent a messenger into town to talk to the bishop. The messenger told the bishop that his leader was very sick and desperately wanted to be converted to Christianity to save his soul before he died. The bishop was super-excited and told Hasting to come right on in; the Viking leader went into the huge church, accepted baptism, then went back to his fleet.

Two days later, the same messenger returned to the bishop. Hasting had died during the night. Would it be okay if they buried him in the church?

Of course, said the bishop.

The next day, a procession of fifty Norsemen in big, loose-fitting robes solemnly walked into the church, carrying a coffin that contained their fallen leader. The bishop waited

for them at the altar to give his sermon and lay Hasting's Christian soul to eternal rest.

When the procession reached the front of the church, however, the coffin lid popped up and Hasting leapt out like a Viking zombie and planted his sword in the bishop. His men threw off their cloaks to reveal that they were decked out in full chain mail and packing enough weaponry to outfit a small army. Things really got ugly in a hurry.

Hasting and his men immediately started running through the streets, waving their swords around willy-nilly and screaming about how they'd just captured Rome, but it turned out they were getting a little overexcited—because oops, guess what, this wasn't Rome. It was just some one-horse Italian town called Luna that nobody outside Italy had ever heard of before. When Hasting figured this out, he got so mad that he ordered the entire population either killed or enslaved. Then he sacked the Italian towns of Pisa, Arno, and Fiesole and wrote some angry poetry before heading off to the eastern Mediterranean, possibly making it as far as Alexandria, Egypt.

Content with their adventures, Hasting and Bjorn Ironside finally headed back to Denmark in 861, their sixty ships completely loaded up with two years' worth of the plundered riches of the Mediterranean.

When they reached the Strait of Gibraltar, they were met with a rude surprise: a full-scale Muslim war fleet that had been built specifically for the purpose of making the Vikings wish they'd never seen a mosque before.

With nowhere to run, Hasting and Bjorn Ironside attacked, charging their ships into the Muslim fleet. Viking longships didn't have any weapons, so the Viking style of naval combat was to crash into the enemy vessel, tie the ships together, then send all the warriors running onto the enemy's boat to kill everyone they could catch.

Unfortunately for the Vikings, the Muslims never let them get that far. They'd developed a secret weapon—the flame-thrower.

Adapted from a weapon invented by the Byzantines (who possibly got it from China), the Muslim flamethrower was a heavy metal tube filled with flammable liquid that was hand-cranked like a Super Soaker—except instead of water, it shot a burning stream of flaming oil that stuck to anything it touched.

Of the sixty ships in Hasting's fleet, only twenty made it through the wall of fire-spewing Muslim warships. On the way home, upset about their defeat and looking for something to vent their Viking rage on, the Norsemen attacked the Spanish town of Pamplona, captured the king of Navarre (a region in northern Spain), and ransomed him for seventy thousand gold coins. The Scandinavians would not attempt another expedition to Spain for four hundred years.

This adventure, however, was an incredible success. When

Hasting and Bjorn Ironside returned home, they were greeted as heroes, and every man in their crew became known as one of the bravest warriors the Viking world had ever seen. Tales of their adventures would be told among skalds for centuries, and their daring raid deep into unknown waters would truly be one of the most amazing adventures of the Viking Age.

Hasting would continue to wreak havoc in Europe, like the time in 869 when he attacked Brittany, the land in the northwest of France, and the people there offered him five hundred cows if he promised to leave them alone. He and Bjorn both also show up in England later on—Bjorn as part of a force that includes his brother Ivar the Boneless in 865, and Hasting with a group that faces off against Alfred the Great in 892—but I'll cover both those tales a little later.

BJORN TO FIGHT

The myth of Bjorn's invincibility mirrors the tale of the legendary Greek warrior Achilles, who was said to have been dipped by his mama into a similar concoction that also made him invincible. In the case of Achilles, his mom held him by the heel when he was dunked into the vat of invincibility serum, which left him a convenient weak point; he was killed by a Trojan archer (named Paris) who managed to put an arrow right in his Achilles tendon (this is how that part of your body got its name), somehow killing him instantly.

ABD AL-RAHMAN

The Muslim emirate in Spain was founded in dramatic fashion by an Arab prince named Abd al-Rahman in 756. Abd was the son of the caliph, ruler of the Muslim world, but a revolution killed every single member of the royal family except Abd, who fled to Damascus, swam a river, and escaped through the Middle East. Abd evaded bands of men seeking to kill him and made his way to Spain, where he linked up with an army of loyal supporters, defeated an army sent by the guys who had killed his dad, and claimed the entire Iberian Peninsula for himself. With a story like that, this guy's descendants weren't going to let Hasting raid their lands without a fight.

SIGURD THE CRUSADER

The Norwegian king Sigurd the Crusader undertook a similar expedition in 1107, but he was interested in battling the Moors for religious purposes. Leading the first Scandinavian army to crusade to the Holy Land, Sigurd raided Moorish and Arab forts and settlements across Spain and North Africa. In one battle, he loaded his archers into a boat and used ropes to lower it into a cave on top of a group of Arab warriors. After a brief stopover in Jerusalem and Constantinople, Sigurd and his men returned to Norway as heroes in 1113.

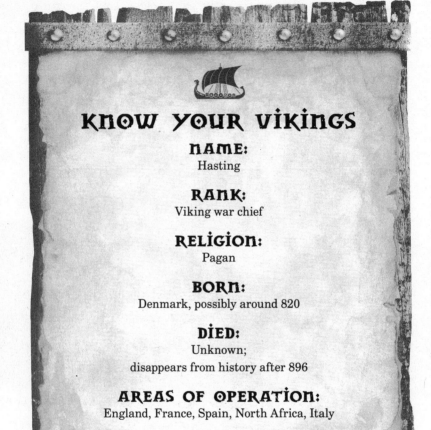

Know Your Vikings

NAME:
Hasting

RANK:
Viking war chief

RELIGION:
Pagan

BORN:
Denmark, possibly around 820

DIED:
Unknown;
disappears from history after 896

AREAS OF OPERATION:
England, France, Spain, North Africa, Italy

NOTEWORTHY:
One of the most successful and ferocious
war leaders in Viking history; led his men
as far as Italy in his quest for plunder

KIEVAN RUS

Vikings settle the Baltic Coast, inadvertently create Russia
c. AD 830–879

Masses of spears and arrows could be seen flying through the air, axes swung violently, shields were split, armor was cut open, helmets were slashed, and skulls were cloven. Many men fell to the ground.

—The Saga of the Volsungs

WE'VE SEEN MARAUDING VIKING CHIEF-tains have their way with towns and countries across Western Europe, create powerful new cities, overthrow kings, and plunder loot by the shipful. But while this was going on, Viking jarls on the other side of Europe were out there doing something even more important for the course of world history.

They were creating the foundation for the country we now know as Russia.

The tale of how a Viking leader named Rurik went from a minor jarl to an all-powerful tsar ("emperor") of Russia starts back in the ninth century, when this sea-marauding warrior and his Viking buddies were having a blast sailing their totally rad dragon-headed longships down the twisting waterways of present-day Eastern Europe. Rurik and his war band had performed many successful raids against the English and Franks, but they became infamous among the local Slavic people for the total devastation they brought with them.

It worked like this: Rurik's group would attack a town, burn it, loot it, and then tie up every able-bodied person who lived there and take them prisoner. They'd then sail down the mighty Dnieper River, past dangers ranging from intense rapids and sharp rocks to bears and bloodthirsty marauders, cross the five-hundred-mile-wide Black Sea, and pull their ships into the Byzantine Empire's capital at Constantinople. The Vikings would sell their captives as slaves; spend their money on weapons, gear, and party supplies; and then head back upriver to do it all over again. The whole thing worked out so well for Rurik that the English word *slave* actually comes from the word *Slav*, the name of the people who lived in Russia at the time (and still do today).

This is pretty messed up, for sure, but the Vikings weren't exactly the sort of people who put a lot of value on human life. For these guys, life was short and difficult, and the strong were there to take what they wanted from the weak. These were big, scary dudes, and nobody wanted them around for very long (for obvious reasons).

Rurik mostly stuck to coastal villages along the Dnieper River and generally left the big cities alone at first. Around this time, the most powerful city in the Slavic world was the wealthy trading town of Novgorod. Defended by imposing city walls and a well-trained army of steel-toed Slavic warriors, Novgorod had been protected from Rurik's raids. But these guys had problems of their own. The short version is that there were three or four groups of powerful noblemen all arguing and fighting over money and power, and things had gotten so out of hand by 860 that corrupt merchants and nobles were having people murdered in back alleys by hardcore hired assassins.

One day, an enterprising Novgorod businessman decided he was going to find a clever way to tip the power struggle in his favor. He sent messengers across Russia to track down the most ferocious human being he could think of—the super-scary Viking leader Rurik. The man whose imposing battle-axe and bad attitude were feared by cowering peasants from Dublin to Constantinople. The last person you'd want to open the gates of your city to.

Apparently unaware that he was dealing with a Viking, the businessman offered Rurik a deal: You come help me take over Novgorod from my two biggest rivals, and we'll split the cash and prizes.

So Jarl Rurik, the notorious plunderer, sea-raider, and all-around scary guy, rolled into town to settle the dispute. He brought with him his two brothers, Sinaus and Truvor, as well as about ten thousand of their closest mead-chugging, axe-swinging buddies.

The other powerful nobles of Novgorod pulled together armies to stop Rurik from entering the city, but it didn't take long for the Vikings to carve their way through their enemies and throw the rival groups out on their butts. Then, seeing the situation that fate had handed him, Rurik figured, "What the heck, while I'm here I'll just take over." So in 862 he seized control of Novgorod, declared himself Iron-Fisted Autocrat Now and Forever, and named his new empire after his Viking tribe: the Rus.

Now, by this point in history, Novgorod was already a highly advanced, incredibly wealthy city that served as a trade hub connecting Europe to the Arab world, the Byzantines, and even the Chinese. Being connected to the world's three wealthiest and most advanced civilizations at this time in history was pretty amazing, and Rurik used the massive amounts of money he was able to bring in to increase the size of his military and go to war with the other Slavic tribes of Russia, the Ukraine, and the Baltic.

For his first conquest, Rurik's troops headed down the Dnieper from Novgorod aboard two hundred longships, where they ran into another powerful Slavic city, Kiev, conquered it, and added it to Rurik's empire.

Rurik's top lieutenants, Askold and Dir, went even farther south, rampaging through the Black Sea in a frenzy of pillaging and sacking, but that party eventually came to an end when they foolishly tried to capture Constantinople itself. You have to admit it took huge guts to try to conquer the world's most heavily fortified city with just a couple hundred determined Vikings, but the Byzantines had a little thing called Greek fire (the Muslims would later use it in their flamethrowers) that made this attack a very bad idea.

Greek fire was a flammable fire-oil that was shot out of ship-mounted flamethrowers and burned so hot that you couldn't even put it out by jumping into the ocean. As soon as you swam to the surface, the oil would catch fire again and keep burning. The recipe for Greek fire is so mysterious that to this day we don't know how they did it. (But it's basically the same as modern-day napalm.)

Engaging the Viking fleet outside the triple walls of Constantinople, the Greeks torched the Norse warships, sending the remaining ships running back to Kiev. Askold and Dir were so impressed by the Byzantine Empire that they converted to Christianity, declared Kiev an Orthodox Christian city-state independent of Novgorodian rule, and rebelled against Rurik. Naturally, Rurik was like, "Okay, jokers, have fun with that," and had them killed and replaced.

Suddenly finding himself a Viking pirate turned world leader, Rurik ruled over Novgorod and Kiev for fifteen years. He built his realm, now known as "Kievan Rus," into the powerful empire that would eventually become Russia. After Rurik's death in 879, his warrior cousin Oleg served as regent for Rurik's four-year-old son, Igor. Igor would eventually take over as ruler, but we'll hear a little more about how that turned out when we get to Saint Olga of Kiev in chapter 14.

Rurik's descendants would conquer even more territory, move their capital to Kiev, and expand Russia from the Baltic to the Black Sea. They dominated the country as iron-fisted tyrants for seven hundred years—a dynasty of all-powerful tsars that lasted until one of them, named Ivan the Terrible, accidentally killed his only son and heir in 1581. It is said that every tsar in history carried with him the same scepter Rurik used to rule over the Novgorodians in 862.

Now, there's a legacy you can be proud of.

THE NAME GAME

Many good, solid Russian names you hear today are derived from the original Norse. For instance, over the years Ingvar became Igor, Helgi became Oleg, Helena became Yelena, Helga became Olga, and Karl just stayed Karl. Tell your friends.

RUNES

The Vikings used a sixteen-letter runic alphabet known as futhark, which is the noise it makes if you read the first couple of letters together. Said to be given to the people by the Norse god Odin, the Norse runes were believed to possess powerful magical capabilities. Warriors would carve words on their blades to give them extra powers or write them on their hands to heal wounds. Pregnant women would carve them on their beds to help with childbirth, and sick people would wear necklaces bearing runes to help cure diseases. Since most Vikings were illiterate, special scribes known as runemasters were responsible for writing the runes, usually by chiseling them into stones or wood with a stick and a hammer.

ᚹᚢᚦᚨᚱᚹ   ᚺᛏᛁᛏᚼ
ᚹᚢᚦᚨᚱᚹ   ᛏᚺᛁᛏᛁ
fuþąrk   hnias
ᛏᛒᚤᚴᛚ
ᛁᚠᛏᚱᛁ
tbmlʀ

Viking runic alphabet   Rune stone in Stockholm, Sweden

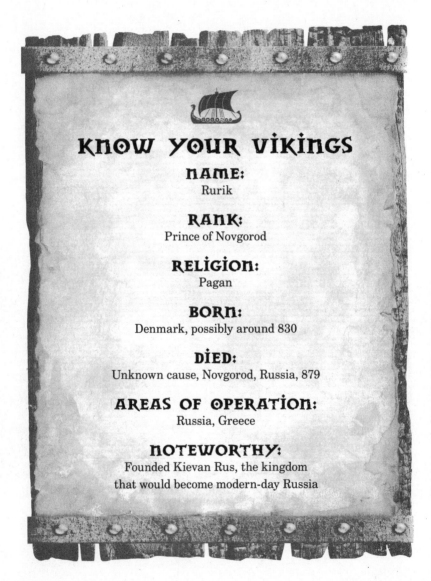

KNOW YOUR VIKINGS

NAME:
Rurik

RANK:
Prince of Novgorod

RELIGION:
Pagan

BORN:
Denmark, possibly around 830

DIED:
Unknown cause, Novgorod, Russia, 879

AREAS OF OPERATION:
Russia, Greece

NOTEWORTHY:
Founded Kievan Rus, the kingdom
that would become modern-day Russia

THE VIKINGS AT HOME

*Home is where the hearth is—
and the lutefisk*

The town is not rich in goods and wealth. The staple food for inhabitants is fish, since it is so plentiful. It often happens that a newborn is tossed into the sea to save raising it. Also, whenever they wish, women may divorce their husbands. An eye makeup used by both men and women causes their beauty never to fade but to increase. But nothing can compare to the dreadful singing of these people, worse even than the barking of dogs.

—Ibrahim ibn al-Tartushi, Muslim adventurer

WITH ALL THE BURNING, LOOTING, plundering, and horrible mutilations going on throughout Europe at the hands of ruthless bands of bloodthirsty Viking pillagers, it's sometimes easy

to lose sight of the fact that most Viking warriors were just
regular folks who lived regular lives. Despite the axe-swinging
mayhem, most of these dudes were just like you or me, only
they didn't talk about video games all day, drink milkshakes,
or have to go to soccer practice. They were farmers, ranchers,
fishermen, and family men, and anytime a Norseman wasn't
out on a raid impaling people and burning their pets, he was
chilling at home, working his day job growing crops or raising
cattle or doing whatever else he had to do to put food on the
table for his family.

A typical day in the life of a non-adventuring Northman
began around six in the morning. The men of the house would
get up, clean their teeth with a wooden twig, and head out into
the fields to work the farm, which wasn't particularly exciting but had to get done anyway. They'd feed the horses, pigs,
sheep, goats, and chickens; sow the fields with flax, wheat,
barley, oats, corn, peas, and cabbage; and do manly things
like fix fences and dig holes. Around eight AM they'd come
back to the house, where the women would have prepared
dagmeal, which is the same thing as breakfast—typically
eggs, buttermilk, salted fish, and maybe some berries or nuts
or veggies. Following the meal, the men would either continue
their work or head out to hunt or fish. Salmon, cod, herring,
and trout were common catches throughout Scandinavia, and
Vikings also hunted deer for food; foxes, wolves, and bears for
their fur; and whales, seals, and walruses, which were prized

for their fatty blubber because that stuff could be used for everything from food to boat grease.

Speaking of fish, a favorite traditional dish for Vikings was lutefisk, a terrible-smelling, jelly-like concoction made from dried, salted cod that's been soaked in lye for so long that it tastes like stinky soap and can probably be classified more as a weapon than a food.

Around seven PM the men would come back home for *nattmeal*—dinner—which the women had been cooking basically since they'd finished making breakfast. *Nattmeal* was an intense feast with honey, beef, fish, cheese, stews, breads, and butter, eaten Viking-style on a wooden plate, with a metal knife and a spoon (but no fork, because forks are for wimps). This was accompanied by a generous helping of ale or mead chugged from the hollowed-out horn of a bull or a ram. In super-rich houses, this meal would sometimes be followed by dancing, singing, acrobats, clowns, and jugglers, and by poets and musicians singing heroic tales of ancient battles before a raging hearth fire.

The Vikings lived in big wooden homes known as longhouses. Ranging from 40 to 250 feet in length and decorated with everything from animal furs to golden cups plundered from French cathedrals, these rectangular homes were handcrafted from wood timbers, then roofed with thick chunks of fresh sod. There were no windows, because windows let in the freezing cold of the Arctic winter, and aside from the front door, the only ventilation was a little chimney hole cut just above a huge fire pit in the middle of the house. There was no electricity, so the fire provided heat, light, and a cooking method, and if you could handle a little smoke inhalation, a good bench near the fire was the best seat in the house. Typically, the longhouse consisted of one or two large rooms, with beds, benches, and tables set up on each side of a long center aisle.

The Vikings lived in longhouses with their entire extended family, including grandparents, uncles, and cousins, and during particularly cold winters, sometimes they'd even bring the dogs and cows and pigs into the house to keep them from freezing to death in the subzero Scandinavian temperatures (the *average* low temperature for winter in Oslo, Norway, is nineteen degrees Fahrenheit...thirteen degrees below freezing!). Those temperatures were not your friend when nature called, because there were no bathrooms in the longhouse. You had to go outside and walk over to your outhouse, which is like a permanent version of those plastic portable bathrooms you see at construction sites and state fairs. When the Vikings were on campaign, they used to have two guys stand outside and guard the outhouse door, because English, Irish, and Frankish peasants liked to kill Vikings while they were trying to go to the bathroom. What a way to go.

Well, all of this was great in the fall and winter, but the average day looked a heck of a lot different in springtime, when every man over the age of fourteen was out gallivanting in Russia and France, laying siege to settlements and lighting villages on fire with flaming arrows and oil-soaked rags. You see, when the men were gone, the Viking women stepped up and took over the day-to-day operation of the houses, towns, and settlements of Scandinavia. They ran the farms and workshops, made clothes, plowed fields, tended crops, and built public works. One still-standing inscription in Gran, Norway, proudly claims GUNNVOR, THRYDRIK'S DAUGHTER, BUILT THIS BRIDGE IN MEMORY OF HER DAUGHTER ASTRID. SHE WAS THE MOST SKILLFUL GIRL IN HADELAND.

It was this strength and independence that provided women in Viking lands far more freedom than women anywhere else in the world at this time. Sure, arranged marriages were common, with most girls being married off between the ages of twelve and fifteen, but if a woman was mistreated by her husband, she was in one of the only civilizations on earth that would allow her to divorce him. What's more, if her husband died, she could remarry whomever she wanted, which was a really forward-thinking concept in 935. This was a time when most other women in the world were still being bought and sold like cattle.

When the Vikings weren't working, drinking, or fighting, they played games and had competitions that more or less resembled some variation of hand-to-hand combat. Swimming competitions were popular. In Viking swimming, you and your buddies swam across a lake in full armor, and it was totally legal to try to drown your opponents by pushing their heads under the water. There were also wrestling matches, in which broken bones were common, and tug-of-war, which was the same as it is today, except instead of a mud pit in the middle, there was a fire pit full of burning-hot coals. If that's a little too dangerous for you, the Vikings also enjoyed spear-throwing competitions and World's Strongest Man–style footraces, where a bunch of guys would pick up a boulder the size of a Prius and run across a field carrying it like a sack of groceries.

One of the most popular spectator sports was horse-fighting, where two angry horses were put in a ring and spectators placed bets on which one would beat up the other one. Vikings also enjoyed ice-skating and skiing, using homemade skates and skis carved from whalebones, and played a board game called Hnefatafl (I have no idea how you'd pronounce it) that was kind of like checkers, except one guy played as the king and his guards, and the other guy played as a war band of marauding Vikings trying to capture and kill him. If none of this sounds like fun, the Vikings also spent quite a bit of time and energy sword fighting with their neighbors over minor transgressions.

In Viking society, each family had to make everything they needed, from food to nails to houses to clothes. Women spun the cloth for the clothes, typically from wool or linen, making long dresses for the girls and knee-length tunics for the boys. Men and women alike wore plenty of jewelry, most of which had been stolen from European churches or castles and was readily available in Scandinavia, and things like gold necklaces, glass beads, and silver armbands were symbols of how successful a family was. Personal hygiene was also pretty big, with saunas being a common fixture, and most Scandinavians bathed about once a week, which was a major deal back in the days before running water and public sewers. Both men and women wore their hair long, with men tying it up in braids to keep it out of their faces and women preferring to wrap it into a bun. Men as well as women wore makeup, using crushed berries for eyeliner, and women sometimes lightened their hair by using bleaching soap.

There were a few large trading towns established by the Vikings—well-known examples being Hedeby in Denmark, York in England, and Dublin in Ireland. Bustling trade towns with ships coming in day and night, these cities were usually protected by wooden or earthen walls and paved with wood-plank or dirt roads. Shipbuilders, blacksmiths, and carpenters worked their trades, and goods were brought in from all around the world—silk from China, leather from Persia (modern-day Iran), steel from Syria, and beaded glass from the Holy Roman Empire could all be found for the right price. In one small village in Sweden, archaeologists unearthed a statue of the Buddha that had been hand-crafted in India—nearly five thousand miles away.

The typical trade routes in the Viking world were undertaken by a group of merchants known as a *félag*—a fellowship, like in *The Lord of the Rings*. These guys would all join forces, promise to divide their income equally, and then head out from Norway or Denmark with a huge trading vessel full of all the good things Scandinavia had to offer—timber, iron, soapstone, sealskin, amber, slaves, falcons, furs, and fish. They'd get Byzantine brocade and Persian spices in Russia; stop in Germany for glass beads and salt; land in France for wine and swords; take those to England and get dyed wool, tin, honey, and silver; then head back home to unload their new wares. If the traders saw another group of merchants on the high seas, they'd swap with them, or if the other trader wasn't particularly well armed, they'd just attack him, kill him, and steal all his stuff. The fellowship would brave harsh storms, avoid roving bands of plunder-seeking pirates, and battle everything from disease to angry villagers in their quest for bargain prices, but for those who returned home with a ship full of exotic materials, there was plenty of money to be made.

THE DANEVIRK

Larger Danish cities and forts were defended by seven-to-eight-foot-high walls (called ramparts) made of raised earth and supported by stacked timbers or stones positioned behind a ditch or moat. These walls would occasionally be tricked out with watchtowers, gates, and palisades (high fences made of pointed stakes), and sharp wooden spikes were placed underwater in the harbor to defend against sea attacks. By far the most impressive of these works was the famous Danevirk. An eighteen-mile-long series of ramparts over twenty feet high, the Danevirk was built around the mid-eighth century to wall off Denmark from the barbarian and Frankish war bands that started kicking around during the age of Charlemagne. Parts of it are still standing today.

I GOTTA GO TO THAT THING

Politics were typically handled at a public assembly known, weirdly enough, as the Thing, where freemen would meet outside at town hall–style meetings to discuss pressing business, settle disputes, pass laws, and vote on land issues. Women were allowed to attend the Thing but could not vote or hold office.

HACK ME OFF SOME SILVER

The Vikings didn't have a centralized form of currency, and they didn't care about the meaningless numbers kings liked to print on the sides of their coins. Only the silver mattered. Each Norse merchant simply carried a set of scales to measure the weight of the coin or item in silver, and calculated its trade value based on that. So, for instance, if both a dime and a nickel were made out of pure silver, the Vikings would give you more for the nickel than the dime. If the merchant didn't have the exact right amount of silver, he'd just chop a chunk off a silver candlestick or plate until he had a piece that was the right weight, a process that led to this form of currency's being referred to as "hacksilver."

THE TOOTH FAIRY

When Viking children lost their baby teeth, it was common for their parents or relatives to give them a piece of candy or a coin to congratulate them. Eventually this practice was joined with the elf- and magic-heavy lore of Viking mythology to create the concept of the Tooth Fairy.

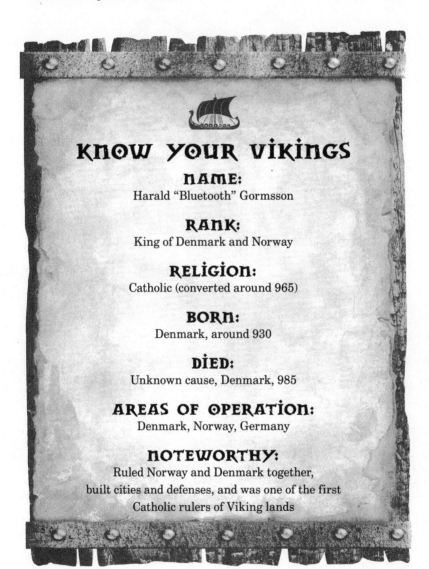

KNOW YOUR VIKINGS

NAME:
Harald "Bluetooth" Gormsson

RANK:
King of Denmark and Norway

RELIGION:
Catholic (converted around 965)

BORN:
Denmark, around 930

DIED:
Unknown cause, Denmark, 985

AREAS OF OPERATION:
Denmark, Norway, Germany

NOTEWORTHY:
Ruled Norway and Denmark together,
built cities and defenses, and was one of the first
Catholic rulers of Viking lands

THE GREAT HEATHEN ARMY

Ivar the Boneless invades England
AD 865–873

> Never before has such a terror appeared in Britain as we have now suffered from a pagan race, nor was it thought that such an inroad from the sea could be made. Behold, the church of Saint Cuthbert spattered with the blood of the priests of God, despoiled of all its ornaments; a place more venerable than all in Britain is given as prey to pagan peoples.
>
> —Alcuin, Anglo-Saxon monk

SINCE THE FIRST BLOODTHIRSTY OUTLAW biker gang of Vikings blitzed into town and helped themselves to the treasures of the monastery at Lindisfarne, things had somehow gotten worse and worse for the poor folks unlucky enough to live in the coastal fishing villages of England. Relentless Viking attacks hammered the shores of the British Isles all the way through the first half of the ninth century, and pretty much every single summer between 798 and 865 saw England dealing with some new group of Viking jerks who would blow into town out of nowhere, kick a puppy or two, wreck everything, and then sail off before the cops or the army showed up.

In the year 865, that snatch-and-grab tradition changed into something far more sinister when a new threat arrived on the shores of England: a fleet of warships unlike anything the Anglo-Saxons had ever seen—black-hulled vessels lined with shields of red and gold, each packed to the brim with big, sweaty Viking warriors intent on bloodshed and the screaming glory of battle.

This was more than a minor Viking raid aimed at snatching a few purses and making off into the sunset.

This was an invasion.

We honestly aren't sure why the Vikings chose 865 as the year they wanted to come ripping across the North Sea on a mission of conquest. Maybe they were just seeking glory and power and the opportunity to exert their ruthless might against a rival kingdom they viewed as soft and weak. Maybe some of the Norse warriors were looking to start a new life far from the frozen tundra of Scandinavia and claim huge chunks of fertile farmland where they could settle down with

their families. Maybe they just had a lot of guys sign up for Viking raids that year and figured, "Hey, what the heck, let's go for it." Historians today aren't certain. And that's partly because the only explanation for the attack comes from the Viking sagas, and their version of the story is so over-the-top nuts that it's a little hard for most folks to believe it.

Remember that I said back in my author's note that Norse history can be hard to write because the Viking sagas include some magical elements that push the border between history and fairy tales? The Great Heathen Army is one of those stories. Basically, the story starts like this: Once upon a time, the most powerful Viking in Denmark was this big, scary guy named Ragnar Hairy-Breeches. Ragnar was a Viking so bone-shatteringly manly that many historians aren't even sure if he was a real person or just some kind of Viking comic-book superhero. Historians who believe he was real suggest that he took part in the Sack of Paris in 845, plundering the richest city in the Western world, but that was hardly his biggest achievement. His claim to fame would be his cool nickname, Hairy-Breeches, which came from the time when he rescued a princess from the clutches of a giant evil serpent by constructing homemade armor and stuffing horsehair down his pants.

According to the saga, this princess was captured by an evil king, who used an enormous, venomous serpent to guard her. Never one to back down from the opportunity to rescue a princess, Ragnar made a pair of awesome leather pants,

lined them with animal hair, dipped it all in tar, and then dunked the whole thing into ice-cold water to harden it up into the sort of thing you probably couldn't resell at a thrift store. Ragnar's rock-hard hair pants did the job, though. They worked like armor to protect him against the poisonous bites of the serpent, and the Viking warrior ended up killing the monster, marrying the princess, and riding off into the sunset. Like I said, Norse sagas are weird.

But it gets better. Ragnar's son was a guy named Ivar the Boneless, who was actually an even more dangerous Viking than his dad. Unlike with Ragnar, we don't know where Ivar got his all-time-great Viking nickname. Some historians think there might have been a mix-up in translation that turned the Latin word *exosus* ("detested") into *exos* ("boneless"). Others say that Ivar had a degenerative musculoskeletal disease that made it difficult for him to stand or walk. This makes sense, because we do know that he didn't travel on foot or by horse. Instead, anytime he wanted to head to the battlefield, he would sit on his shield and have four big Viking dudes carry him.

Since he wasn't your everyday axe-swinging Viking warrior, Ivar had to use his cunning, wits, and intelligence to lead his armies to glory. And he was pretty good at it. During the 850s, he led dozens of raids up and down the British Isles, and eventually took over as ruler of Dublin in Ireland after Turgeis the Devil got himself tortured and thrown into a lake to drown.

Now, if the stories are to be believed (and they probably aren't), Ivar became so popular that his dad, Ragnar Hairy-Breeches, started getting insecure and jealous of his son's fame. So he decided to one-up Ivar with a daring move—he would take a mere three ships full of Viking warriors and personally conquer the entire English kingdom of Northumbria.

This was a stupid plan, and it shouldn't surprise you to hear that it failed miserably. As soon as Ragnar unloaded his ships on the shores of Northumbria, a guy named King Aella showed up, destroyed Ragnar's forces, and killed the Viking warrior by throwing him into a pit filled with poisonous snakes. Ivar responded by becoming obscenely enraged and deciding to avenge his father at the head of a fleet so massive that the Anglo-Saxon Chronicle (the earliest known history of England) refers to it simply as "the Great Heathen Army."

As I said, that backstory is probably about as historically accurate as Disney's portrayal of Pocahontas, so don't take it too seriously. It doesn't really matter *why* they came across the sea. What matters is what they did once they got there.

They kicked butt.

Charging through the crashing waves, axes and torches held high, the Vikings raced from their ships into the country-side of the kingdom of Northumbria and immediately started laying waste to the land. And while King Aella could handle a trio of warships led by a delusional old Viking warlord on a suicide mission, he was a lot less prepared to be on the receiving end of an epic Viking beatdown. By the time he built up an organized force and was ready to fight, Ivar the Boneless had already sacked a dozen villages, wiped out a few military garrisons, captured the walled city of York, and set it up as a base of operations so he could bring in more men and supplies from Denmark. York would stand as a Viking stronghold for the next hundred years.

The Northumbrian king massed his troops and attacked Ivar outside the towering stone walls of York, but it was too little, too late. Waves of brave English fighters stormed the fortress city in a heroic attack, but what little progress they made was crushed by the Viking shield wall. Ivar the Boneless and his bloodthirsty men drove back the English assault, counterattacked, sent the English armies scattering into the countryside, killed several members of the Northumbrian aristocracy, and captured the notorious King Aella.

Remembering that this guy was the one who'd supposedly had Ivar's dad nibbled to death by a vat full of tiny snakes, Ivar the Boneless ordered that King Aella be put to death by "Blood Eagle." And for those of you who aren't down with ninth-century torture methods, Blood Eagle is the cool-sounding Viking term for a process that I'd assume has to rank very high on the list of most horrific ways a human being can be killed. The Vikings, in their infinite knowledge of how much punishment a human body can take before croaking, apparently discovered a way to kill people by pulling their lungs out through their backs while they were still alive. In addition to scaring the pants off their enemies, the Vikings also did this as a sacrifice to Odin, who seems to have appreciated that sort of thing.

King Aella understandably didn't survive without his

lungs for very long, but he was really just one of four guys who had lands in England in 865. Far from being a unified island (although it would become one by the time the Vikings were done with it), the place we know as England today was actually four separate kingdoms then: Northumbria, Mercia, East Anglia, and Wessex—each with its own king.

Now that he had taken Northumbria, Ivar intended to smash the other three.

Operating out of his home base in York, Northumbria—a region beginning to be known to the English as the "Danelaw" (because it was subject to the law of the Danes)—Ivar the Boneless coordinated a massive assault on all things English. As soon as winter was over, he raided the kingdom of Mercia, destroying its army and only agreeing to leave town after the king of Mercia bought him off with giant donkey carts full of gold and jewels. Ivar's Viking marauders then rampaged to the south, where they annihilated the forces of yet another English ruler, King Edmund of East Anglia. Edmund was a hardcore ultra-religious Christian, and even after his army was stomped into fertilizer, the king refused to surrender because he didn't want to submit to a non-Christian, Odin-worshipping heathen.

So Ivar the Boneless captured Edmund by force, tied him to a tree, had his archers use the king for target practice, and then cut off his head and threw it in a hole. The Catholic Church declared Edmund a martyr and made him into Saint

Edmund, which was a nice consolation prize. Saint Edmund's vengeance-loving ghost will later be credited with killing another invader from Denmark, Svein Forkbeard, 150 or so pages from now, in chapter 19.

So now Ivar the Boneless and the Great Heathen Army were in a really good spot. They'd conquered East Anglia and Northumbria, and ruled the eastern part of the English island with an iron fist, dominating their subjects and bringing in more troops and supplies from Denmark on a daily basis. Mercia, to the west of York, had been pummeled into submission and was dishing out its lunch money to avoid being beaten up by Vikings.

Ivar left the conquest of the fourth kingdom, Wessex, to his lieutenant Guthrum (I'll deal more with Guthrum in the next chapter), so this is pretty much where Ivar's story ends. Content with conquering most of England in a flurry of axe blows to the dome, Ivar retired from a life of dismembering people and went back to rule from his dual castles in York and Dublin. He died around 873 from unknown causes—he either passed peacefully on his farm or was stabbed to death by Irishmen while leading a raid.

One thing that's certain is that England would never be the same. Ivar had entered an island kingdom divided by four factions all bitterly fighting one another. His actions, and those of the Great Heathen Army, started a process that would unite the four kingdoms into England as we know it today.

THE DANELAW

Ivar's victories established what became known as the Danelaw—a large section of northeastern England that was settled and ruled by the Danes. Despite the best efforts of the English to crush this pesky, Viking-infested portion of their island, the Danelaw existed throughout the Viking Age and wasn't fully erased from the map until after William the Conqueror came by in 1066.

THE MOO OF INSANITY

One saga story claims that Ivar defeated an enemy army that had a deadly secret weapon—a giant evil cow whose horrific Moo of Insanity made warriors freak out and start randomly killing one another. Ivar outsmarted the beast by sitting down on his shield and having his men hurl him at the creature, plowing into it in a righteous midair collision and knocking both of them down a hill and out of the battle. Ivar's men were so psyched the cow was gone that they ran in and won the fight.

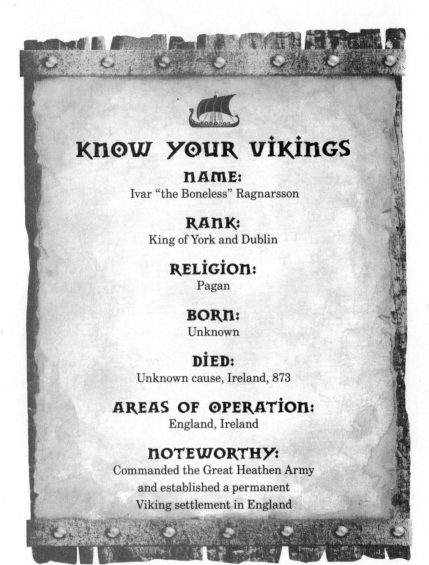

KNOW YOUR VIKINGS

NAME:
Ivar "the Boneless" Ragnarsson

RANK:
King of York and Dublin

RELIGION:
Pagan

BORN:
Unknown

DIED:
Unknown cause, Ireland, 873

AREAS OF OPERATION:
England, Ireland

NOTEWORTHY:
Commanded the Great Heathen Army
and established a permanent
Viking settlement in England

BRITAIN FIGHTS BACK

Alfred the Great makes a stand
against the Viking horde
AD 870–918

Against England the Jarl urged his banner;
Oft his war band blooded the hawk-beak;
Fire shrank the halls as the folk ran,
Flame ravaged, smoke reared, reeking skyward.

—Arnor Jarlaskald, Viking skald

WITH THE GREAT HEATHEN ARMY
of Viking marauders ruthlessly ravaging the
English countryside, the ultimate salvation of
the land rested on the sword arm of one young prince: a hero
who was destined to save his people and his kingdom from

ultimate destruction at the bloody hands of the Norsemen. A man with the strength, ingenuity, dedication, and intelligence to stand tall against the Viking horde. A man who would engage them at their own game and turn the tables with a ferocious determination they hadn't experienced since the days of Charlemagne.

When he was born, he was fifth in line to the throne of the kingdom of Wessex. By the time he died, he would be the only English ruler to be known by the epithet "the Great."

Born in Wantage, Berkshire, Alfred was a prince of Wessex, a kingdom in the south of England. When the Great Heathen Army attacked, he was just sixteen years old, but he was the strongest and most capable military commander his kingdom had to offer. Leading troops in the name of his only surviving brother, King Ethelred of Wessex, Alfred rallied the peasant militias to stand against the onslaught of the Great Heathen Army.

Commanding from the front and personally crashing into Viking formations at the head of his vaunted "household cavalry," the young prince engaged the Vikings in no fewer than seven full-scale battles during the year 871 alone. In most of these battles, his unarmored, spear-wielding peasant militias took a beating at the hands of the Vikings, but every time he was defeated, Alfred managed to withdraw with his army intact, reposition them to block the Viking advance, and hit the invaders again, continually wearing them down. Finally, at the Battle of Ashdown, Alfred caught the Viking warrior Halfdan's forces unaware and led a charge that crippled his army, killing five Danish jarls and a minor Viking king with an unpronounceable name (Bagsecg). The battle sent the Great Heathen Army reeling, and without the manpower to replenish its ranks, Halfdan accepted an offer of cash to get out of Wessex and leave Alfred alone.

Three months after the victory at Ashdown, King Ethelred died, and the crown passed to young Alfred.

Alfred barely had time to move his stuff into the palace before the Vikings were up to their old tricks. In 875, eager to grab more land for himself and his followers, a Viking warrior named Guthrum (who hadn't been in on all that "please leave us alone" money Alfred had paid Halfdan) assembled an army, snuck his warriors past Alfred's forts and watchtowers, put together a fleet to attack by sea, and launched a mega-full-scale raid to destroy the kingdom of Wessex once and for all. Caught off guard, Alfred raced to face Guthrum, but his forces were crushed and he barely escaped the battle with his life by turning his horse and sprinting out of there in a very unkingly fashion. Most of his subjects believed their king had either fallen in battle or deserted them as a coward.

Running for his life, King Alfred of Wessex fled into the

swamps and marshes of Somerset with only a handful of his most trusted bodyguards. Beyond the swamps, Guthrum ravaged the countryside with impunity, pillaging, plundering, and torching Alfred's loyal subjects without mercy. Hopeless towns and villages submitted to the Vikings without a fight and had their populations sold into slavery for their troubles.

Things had gotten bad. One story claims that Alfred sought refuge in the home of an old peasant woman who lived in a little hut in the middle of the Somerset swamp, and that the woman, not knowing she was addressing her rightful king, said that in exchange for lodging he had to keep an eye on the oven while she was cooking some cakes and pies. Alfred, probably a little preoccupied with the Viking invasion, forgot to do this, and the old lady yelled at him for letting her cakes burn.

Not exactly a high point in the life of King Alfred the Great. But don't think for a second that this guy was about to just roll over and call it quits. He was going to fight until his dying day.

In 876, King Alfred of Wessex emerged from the swamps, walked to the nearest city, and headed straight to the town square. Pulling out his best royal pump-up speech, he told the people that he was their king and that any man who wanted to defend his home, his kingdom, and his family from ultimate destruction at the hands of bloodthirsty Viking raiders should rally to their king and prepare for the fight of their lives.

From Somerset, Wiltshire, Hampshire, and all across Wessex, ordinary peasant farmers, mercenaries, fishermen, hunters, and other regular guys grabbed the spears, axes, pitchforks, and shovels out of their garages and marched to join their king.

At the Battle of Edington in 878, King Alfred the Great approached Guthrum's ever-triumphant Viking horde at the head of an army of twenty-five hundred peasant citizen-soldiers

ready to defend their land or die trying. The Viking army assembled their shield wall, preparing for a slaughter. The men of Wessex met them with a ferocity that can only come from men defending their families and their way of life.

All Alfred's chronicler has to say on the subject is that the king "overthrew the pagans with great slaughter, and, smiting the fugitives, he pursued them."

Screaming into battle, the peasant armies hacked with woodcutters' axes and homemade spears, broke through Guthrum's shield wall, and split his forces. As the Vikings turned to flee, their units in tatters, Alfred pursued Guthrum and his men all the way to the nearest town, surrounded them, and besieged them for two weeks. Running out of food, and with nowhere to go, Guthrum surrendered. Alfred allowed him to live and to rule over a portion of the land he had conquered, but only if Guthrum converted to Christianity and signed a treaty swearing never to return to Wessex. Guthrum agreed. Alfred personally stood as his sponsor at the baptism, and Guthrum, to his credit, did a very un-Viking thing and kept his word. He changed his name to Aethelstan, printed coins with his face on them, built churches, and settled down to rule as a legitimate king instead of a mass-murdering Viking maniac.

The Danes still held most of England, but Alfred's control over Wessex was complete, and he went to work protecting

his borders against any future attacks. He built a huge net-
work of fortresses, revamped his army so that it could react
much more quickly, and ordered the construction of a special
fleet of ships specifically designed to fight Viking longships.
He attacked and recaptured London from the Vikings, built
forts to blockade the river Thames against invaders, and
strengthened his position by marrying the princess of Mercia
and uniting the two surviving British kingdoms into one
unified English front. The Vikings were so unnerved by the
whole thing that they left the island alone for a while, attacking the Franks on the mainland of Europe instead.

When a Viking fleet finally returned to assault England in
892, Alfred the Great was ready. He'd spent the past fourteen
years preparing for this moment.

A massive black-hulled fleet of eighty dragon ships
appeared at the mouth of the Thames under command of our
old friend Hasting, the Viking warrior who had pillaged Italy
thirty years earlier. Hasting—now an old man looking for
one more great victorious raid to add to his already incalcu-
lable glory—parked his ships in the harbor at a town called
Benfleet and led his warriors screaming into the countryside
to terrorize the hapless peasantry.

Alfred the Great instantly raised an army of peasant
militias, snuck around the Vikings, stormed the fortress of
Benfleet in record time, massacred the Danish garrison,

burned the Vikings' ships, and captured the wives and children the Vikings had brought along with them. In a poetic
reversal of fortune, Hasting had to pay a ransom to get his
wife and kids back, and Alfred only granted it when the
Vikings promised to get the heck out of there and never
return.

Some people never learn, however, and this humiliating
defeat only made the Vikings even more upset. But every
time they tried to strike out for revenge, they ran into a stone
wall named Alfred the Great. In 893, they attacked through
Wales into Mercia. Alfred couldn't get an army up there fast
enough to stop them, so he ordered that all the crops and
food in West Mercia be burned. The Vikings, unable to for-
age food from the countryside, were forced to turn back. In
895, they sailed a fleet to threaten London, but a British fleet
blockaded the river behind them, cutting off their only escape
route, and the Vikings were forced to abandon their boats and
run for it when they heard that Alfred was charging in their
direction at the head of an army of three thousand screaming British dudes. In 896, an attack on the Wessex coastline
was thwarted, and then, as the Vikings were fleeing in their
ships, Alfred caught up to them with his own fleet, destroyed
them in a naval battle, crippled six of their boats, and hanged
their crews as pirates.

King Alfred the Great of Wessex, once reduced to burning
cupcakes in a swamp, was now firmly in control of a hardened

kingdom capable of hurling back any Viking who would dare threaten him. When Alfred died in 899, Wessex was not only safe but also in a position to take the fight back to the Viking hordes and reconquer England for the Anglo-Saxons.

‹ ‹ ‹

INVADING THE INVADERS

As much as the Anglo-Saxons liked to think of England as their home turf, those guys weren't exactly natives, either. They'd originally come from Germany and Denmark in the middle of the fifth century and killed off or intermingled with the native Briton, Pict, and Celtic populations, forming the basis of English culture as we know it today.

BEOWULF

It was around this time that the Anglo-Saxon epic poem *Beowulf* was written. Dated somewhere between the eighth and eleventh centuries, *Beowulf* is a heartwarming tale about a Swedish guy who gets naked, rips the arm off a man-eating demon, kills that demon's mom at the bottom of a swamp, becomes king, kills a dragon, and dies on top of a pile of money. Not surprisingly, this story has sold quite a few copies in the past twelve hundred years.

THE RECONQUEST
OF ENGLAND

Alfred the Great was succeeded by his son Edward the
Elder, who inherited a hardcore Wessex army specifically
designed to destroy Vikings. Edward allied with his sister
Aethelflaed, whom Alfred had installed as queen of Mercia,
and together the two kingdoms united and went on the
offensive.

Their first threat was actually an internal one. Their
cousin Ethelwold, son of the long-dead King Ethelred
of Wessex, thought he should have been king instead of
Edward. Maybe he did have a legit claim on the position, but
that certainly wasn't going to happen, and when Ethelwold
made an alliance with the Vikings to help him kill Edward,
he pretty much signed his own death warrant. Edward and
Aethelflaed crushed him in 903 in a gigantic battle that left
eight Viking jarls and the would-be king Ethelwold dead on
the battlefield.

From this point on, King Edward and Queen Aethelflaed
marched on a ruthless, unstoppable bro-sis assault to retake
England from the Vikings. They wore down Viking warriors in battle after battle, crushing them on the field and
building impenetrable fortresses on top of their corpses.
The Vikings, many of whom had stopped raiding and
started settling the land, were deprived of their greatest

weapon—their mobility—and with none of the jarls united under one leader, they were taken apart piece by piece as the "Lady of the Mercians" and Edward the Elder stormed city after city in their epic quest.

By Aethelflaed's death in 918, the brother-sister team ruled over all England south of the Humber River. By 930, the kingdom of Wessex would throw the last Viking jarl out of England. The Vikings wouldn't return for another seventy years.

KNOW YOUR
VIKING HISTORY

NAME:
Alfred "the Great"

RANK:
King of England

RELIGION:
Catholic

BORN:
Wantage, England, April 23, 871

DIED:
Died of illness, Winchester,
England, October 26, 899

AREA OF OPERATION:
England

NOTEWORTHY:
Defeated the Vikings in England; was the only
English king ever to be known as "the Great"

HARALD FAIRHAIR

The hero-king of Norway and his amazing hair
AD 880–930

> She has reminded me of those things which it now seems strange I have not thought of before. And I make this vow, and the god who made me and rules all things shall be my witness, that never shall my hair be cut or combed till I have possessed myself of all Norway in scot, dues, and rule—or else die.
>
> —King Harald Fairhair

HARALD FAIRHAIR WAS THE FIRST TRUE king of Norway, the national hero of his country, and a man known not only for a mighty propensity for carving through his enemies like a Thanksgiving turkey but also for rocking a head of epically glorious hair so righteous it's the primary way violence-loving Viking skalds chose to remember his name.

Seeing as how this guy never really bothered to write anything down, many of the details of Harald's reign are cloaked in mythology, folklore, and hopefully true anecdotes about his incredible feathered mullet. We know for sure that he was a real guy, that he was the first king of Norway, and that he founded a dynasty that would rule the northern Viking lands off and on throughout the entire Viking Age. Which is enough on its own, I suppose.

But his story is too good not to tell in a little more detail. So for that we go to the sagas, one of which was written by a guy named Hornklove, which is awesome.

As I've mentioned previously, Norway wasn't actually a country or a kingdom back in the 800s. Known simply as the "North Way," this part of the Scandinavian peninsula was really just a mishmash of minor Viking kingdoms, each ruled by a different guy. There was no national identity, no overarching king, and no Norwegian Olympic downhill-skiing team—it was all just a loosely associated group of crown-wearing bearded dudes ruling little towns and villages and generally just pretending they were a heck of a lot more important than they actually were.

Young Harald Fairhair came from a long line of these minor kings, and for some reason most of his grandpas met gruesome, untimely, and historically unlikely ends. One great-

great-great-granddaddy passed out and drowned in a vat of mead. Another was captured by the Swedish and offered to the gods as a human sacrifice. One was burned alive. Another was supposedly attacked in his bed and suffocated by demons. Most met their ends the old-fashioned Viking way, either dying in combat or being murdered by their brothers, cousins, neighbors, or wives.

The most recent fatality in the unlucky history of Harald Fairhair's genealogy was his pops, Halfdan the Black, who drowned when the Santa Claus–style sleigh he was driving crashed through the thin ice of a partially thawed lake and dumped him into freezing-cold water. Harald was ten years old when this happened. Now he was the ruler of the small kingdom of Vestfold.

As you can probably imagine, your typical big, strapping Viking warrior wasn't exactly thrilled about the idea of having to take orders from a ten-year-old kid who hadn't even grown a decent beard yet, so a lot of Vestfold's jarls rose up and tried to yank power away from Harald. Luckily for the young king, he had a secret weapon—his father's chief military advisor and captain of the Vestfold royal guard was a warmongering human killing machine known as Duke Guthorm. Together with Guthorm, Harald (who was, it turned out, a whole lot tougher than his enemies expected) responded to the jarls' insubordination by mobilizing his troops and preparing for war.

His first opponent was King Gandalf—yes, you read that correctly, Tolkien fans—who tried to act quickly and seize power right away, before Harald could organize. But Harald wasn't the sort of guy who hesitated, ever. He and Guthorm got the drop on Gandalf's army, ambushed them, cut off their escape, and killed both Gandalf and his son in a single battle. ("You shall not pass!") Then, when he heard some other guy was trying to overthrow him, the young king sent Viking warriors to sneak into that dude's city and set fire to his castle in the middle of the night. When the wannabe future king and his men ran outside to escape the blaze, they fled right into the spears of Harald Fairhair's warriors.

A few years later, after cementing his power, Harald Fairhair decided he wanted to get married, so he sent his men to talk to the princess of a neighboring kingdom called Hordaland. The princess, whose name was Gyda, was like, "Yeah, I don't think so." She told Harald's men she was worthy of a mighty kingdom like the kingdom of Gorm the Old, who had united all of Denmark, or like the kingdom of Erik Weatherhat (yes, Weatherhat), who had united Sweden a few years back, and if this Harald dude was so marriage-worthy, how come all he had was some puny little nothing kingdom?

When Harald's men came back and relayed her message to their king, they politely asked if they should just burn down her castle and carry her away against her will, but the king said no. He liked her spirit. He would be the man she deserved. He would rule Norway as one kingdom.

That day, King Harald of Vestfold swore he would not cut or comb his hair until he had accomplished his epic mission— the conquest of every minor kingdom in Norway.

Very little is known of the bloody ten-year campaign that ensued, except that no man could stand against the furious might of Harald's ridiculous, never-ending hair. With his long, flowing locks blowing in the breeze behind him, the king charged across the coastal districts and waterways of Norway, into the Uplands, across dales and tundras, winning battle after battle, conquering obscure kingdom after obscure kingdom, destroying all who dared oppose him. Outside Trondheim, he defeated eight kings in eight battles to seize the city. Another time, he killed three enemy kings in a single battle when they tried to team up against him. Before long, enemy kings were running the white flag up their castle walls as soon as they saw Harald's banners fluttering in the breeze.

Unstoppable, strong-willed, and energetic, King Harald was also fair. He respected and upheld the laws passed at the Things (the parliaments held by the people) and left the jarls alone to run their territory untouched. He only asked for two things: (1) He placed a land tax on the freemen, demanding they pay him for the privilege of being his subjects. The jarls collected the money, kept one-third of it (which made them happy), and gave the rest to Harald. And (2) from the jarls, Harald demanded sixty warriors for the national army, plus an additional twenty men from each of the jarl's *hersirs*. This wasn't too tough—men who'd heard the great tales of Harald's dominating victories came from every corner of Norway, Denmark, and Sweden to seek glory, treasure, and excitement fighting for the hero-king and his dreadlocked, uncombed mega-hair and matching floor-length beard. Before long, Harald became known for personally charging into combat at the head of a super-scary force of Viking berserkers.

Eventually, all of Norway was divided into two factions— the kingdom of Harald Fairhair and a huge alliance of Norwegian rulers who would rather have been kings of tiny kingdoms than subordinates of Harald. At the Battle of Hafrsfjord around 880, Harald Fairhair sailed his fleet into

a fjord and crashed his ships into an enemy armada commanded by rulers with names like Solvi Bandy-Legs, Kjotvi
the Rich, Tore Hagalang, and Hadd the Hard. Harald's sail-
ors latched their boats to their foes' and unloaded shiploads
of berserkers. Men battled hard across the decks of the ships,
which burned and sank and broke apart, filling the harbor
with shredded masts, broken shields, and terrified enemy
warriors in full armor swimming for their lives. The battle
was hard fought, lasted all day, and left lots and lots of men
at the bottom of the fjord.

At the end of the day, Harald Fairhair stood atop the
prow of his dragon-headed longship, surveying the ultimate
destruction of the enemy fleet. After ten years of war, he had
finally conquered.

Harald, who at this point was named Harald Tanglehair
thanks to his rat's nest of a head, finally cut his hair. Everyone
was so impressed with his new hairstyle that he immediately
became known as Harald Fairhair, or, alternately, Harald
Greathair. He married Princess Gyda and had five kids with
her, but thanks to his movie-star good looks, women from all
over the place were falling in love with him the second they
saw him, and Gyda was one of something like ten women who
bore him somewhere between sixteen and twenty kids during
his lifetime. His favorite of these wives was Ragnhild the
Mighty, a princess of Denmark who captured Harald's heart so
intensely that he divorced nine women, including Gyda, before

he married her. (Sorry, babe, you had your chance to get in on the ground floor of this thing.)

As king of Norway, Harald Fairhair went to work defending his borders and his kingdom against enemies from across the North Sea. Most of his foes, seeking to flee his wrath, had moved to Iceland or to the Shetland or Orkney Islands or the Hebrides off the coast of Scotland in a desperate mass exodus. But now they were using their old Viking tricks to launch longship raids on Harald's territory in the summers.

This wouldn't fly. Harald responded by sending fleets to all these places and laying waste to anyone who would dare authorize a Viking raid on Norway. Before long, people chilled out.

Harald Fairhair ruled Norway as a just and powerful king for over fifty years, dying around 933 at the age of eighty-three. Today he is revered as the founder of his country, the greatest king in Norwegian history, and a central figure of the Viking era. He was buried on the grounds of his favorite palace, and today his epic victory at Hafrsfjord is marked by one of the most hardcore monuments ever—a set of three gigantic Viking-style swords, each measuring over thirty feet tall, embedded side by side in the rocky cliff overlooking the fjord where the battle was fought.

EYVIND THE PLAGIARIST

Eyvind Skaldaspillir was the court skald (poet) for Harald's son, Haakon the Good, in the tenth century. Although known to history as Eyvind the Plagiarist, this poet and writer probably much preferred the literal translation of his nickname, "Eyvind, the Destroyer of Skalds." Very little of his work remains, so people typically like to interpret "destroyer of skalds" to mean that he was ripping everyone off, but there's a slight chance that he was so incredibly good at what he did that every other writer in Viking Norway wanted to take a pen to their eyes because they'd never be better than Eyvind. Either way, he was still good enough that he got to keep his job after Haakon was usurped by Harald Greycloak, and nowadays he's mentioned in the second verse of the Norwegian national anthem.

GORM THE OLD

The unification of Denmark was completed in a similar fashion by the Danish warrior-king Gorm the Mighty, who raised a huge army in the mid-tenth century, destroyed his enemies, and ruled so long that by the time he died, everyone was just calling him Gorm the Old. Gorm's son Harald Bluetooth would consolidate the power of the Danish crown, building fortresses and towers across the countryside to defend his people from Viking raids, Saxon war bands, and Holy Roman Empire invasions alike.

THE FOUNDING
OF ICELAND

The first Viking to spot Iceland was a semi-legendary guy named Gardar the Swede, who sort of just ran into the island by accident after he was blown off course on his way to the Hebrides. Gardar sailed around the tiny North Atlantic island, named it Gardarsholm after himself, and then promptly left and never returned.

A few years later, a dude named Naddod accidentally discovered Iceland for the second time, saw there was nobody there, and then ended up having to stay the entire winter because a bunch of bad storms kept him from getting his ship back to sea. Bitter, freezing, and angry, Naddod named the island Snowland and promised never to come back.

The next Viking to try his luck was a lovable little adventurer named Floki, who set sail from the Faeroe Islands north of Scotland with a group of colonists, some livestock, and three ravens. After he'd been at sea awhile, he let one of the ravens go, and it flew back to the Faeroes. He waited a little longer, then let the second raven go, but that one couldn't find a good spot to land, so it came back to his ship. Finally, after sailing even farther, Floki let the third raven go, and that one spotted Iceland and flew right to it. Floki followed the raven and landed his crew on the new, largely unexplored land, and everyone was so psyched, they started calling him Floki Raven. However, the thrill surrounding the third Viking discovery of Iceland soon faded when people realized Floki wasn't nearly as good at actually building a colony as he was at collecting ravens. When winter came on unexpectedly, all Floki's cattle died, his crops failed, and his people had to suffer through a miserable time during which they spent most of their time coming up with much ruder nicknames for their fearless leader. Once summer came around and it was warm enough to sail, Floki and his crew bolted, and when they got back to the Faeroes, he told everyone the new name of the place was Iceland.

The Vikings finally got it right on the fourth try, and they did it in a very Viking way—when Ingolf Arnason and his foster brother, Sword-Leif, had to flee Norway because they had killed some guys who were flirting with Sword-Leif's wife. Outlawed by King Harald Fairhair, Ingolf and Sword-Leif loaded up a longship, plundered the northern coast of Ireland, then set up the first permanent settlement in Iceland along with their families, some colonists, and a large group of Irish slaves.

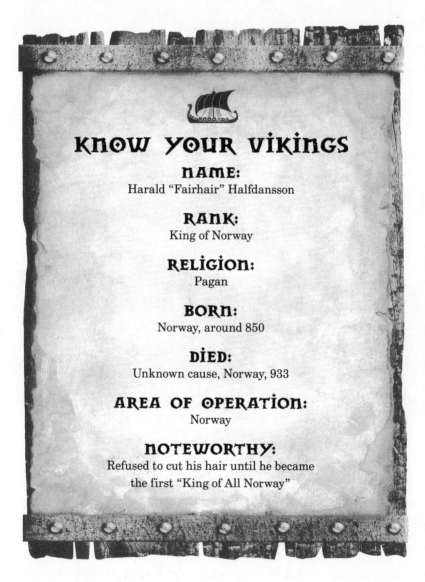

KNOW YOUR VIKINGS

NAME:
Harald "Fairhair" Halfdansson

RANK:
King of Norway

RELIGION:
Pagan

BORN:
Norway, around 850

DIED:
Unknown cause, Norway, 933

AREA OF OPERATION:
Norway

NOTEWORTHY:
Refused to cut his hair until he became
the first "King of All Norway"

GUNNHILD, MOTHER OF KINGS

The ambition and brutality of
Queen Gunnhild Kingsmother
c. AD 900–970

A most beautiful woman, wise and learned, gladsome of speech, but very guileful and stern in disposition.

—Snorri Sturluson, *Heimskringla*

JUST BECAUSE THEY WEREN'T ALWAYS LEAPING from the decks of burning longships and swinging their mighty broadswords at a mob of fleeing peasants, that doesn't mean Viking women weren't some of the toughest, most independent, most ferocious, and most utterly ruthless human beings ever to walk the earth. Coming from a civilization that was unusually good to women compared with elsewhere in the world, Viking women owned property, built structures, managed farms, and basically ran the show while their husbands were gone for months or even years at a time on their epic raids. The self-reliance and strength required to keep their families alive in a harsh, subzero tundra environment surrounded by Vikings made the Norse women fierce, bold, and daring...and more than a match for their axe-swinging husbands and sons in matters of personal courage and intelligence.

Of those daring, no-nonsense Norse women, none was more fierce—or notorious—than the infamous Gunnhild, Mother of Kings. Wife, mother, and daughter of powerful Viking rulers, two-time queen of Norway, and a well-spoken political animal, this woman was also so despised for her cruelty that saga writers portray her less like a historical figure and more like a wicked witch from an antiquated fairy tale.

Sources differ on where Gunnhild came from, but the best guess is that she was a daughter of Gorm the Old, the powerful Viking king who had spent his apparently exceptionally long life conquering most of the small kingdoms of Denmark and uniting them into one land. Gorm was basically the Harald Fairhair of Denmark, and by the time both those guys were done killing everyone who disagreed with them, all the Viking lands had gone from being a bunch of tiny nothing kingdoms to two really powerful ones—Norway and Denmark. Naturally, the best thing to do was to unite those two countries through marriage. So Gorm the Old's daughter Gunnhild was sent to Norway to marry Harald Fairhair's son Erik. This would, in theory, unify the land under one Viking king, and everyone would live happily ever after in one jolly sing-along filled with helmets and axes and burning and destruction.

Unfortunately, things didn't work out that way (they usually don't).

For starters, Princess Gunnhild was not your typical glass-slipper-wearing Disney princess with a blindingly white smile and one of those little waves the beauty queens do on TV. Sure, she was legendarily beautiful, eloquent, and really fun to talk to at parties, but she was also calculating, ambitious, and deadly. According to one (highly unreliable) source, she'd spent part of her life living in a hut near the North Pole, learning magic from two Finnish sorcerers, only to have them murdered once she'd become more powerful than them. While the whole witchcraft-and-magic thing was probably bogus, it is true that Gunnhild didn't take talk-back from anybody, and she didn't hesitate to go for the jugular to get what she wanted.

Gunnhild's husband was a nice, handsome prince named Erik Bloodaxe. Yes, Bloodaxe.

Erik was the favorite son of King Harald Fairhair, and after Fairhair retired from being king in the late 920s, he passed the throne to Erik and Gunnhild, who were crowned king and queen of Norway. Of course, as I mentioned before,

Harald Fairhair had *a lot of kids*, and this king/queen thing didn't sit well with Erik's *twenty* half brothers, all of whom wanted that crown for themselves. When Harald died a couple of years later, Erik's brothers decided they were going to do something about it.

Luckily for Erik Bloodaxe, he had a secret weapon—his wife. Queen Gunnhild, signing secret backroom treaties, buying off corrupt politicians, and outright hiring professional assassins and poisoners, immediately went to work making sure nobody even dreamed of taking the crown of Norway from the head of her beloved husband. One by one, and for various reasons, Erik Bloodaxe's half brothers began

passing out of history. One of them tried to make an alliance against Erik, so Gunnhild had him locked inside his own house, which was then set on fire. Another brother picked a fight with Erik over a land dispute, so Gunnhild paid a witch to poison him. She got one brother, Haakon the Good, deported to England. Another was completely discredited and abandoned by his own followers after some nasty rumors about him started spreading.

Eventually, with brothers dropping off all over the place, things got so out of control that all the sons of Harald Fairhair raised armies and fought it out in a huge battle on a giant snowy field near Erik's palace. Four separate armies, each commanded by a Fairhair son, met in a swirling, bloody melee that left thousands of brave Vikings dead on the field. From the rubble, smoke, destruction, and carnage, only one side emerged victorious—that of Erik Bloodaxe and his wife, Queen Gunnhild.

Things went great for a while. Erik Bloodaxe and Queen Gunnhild ruled with an iron fist, kept the jarls in line, eviscerated anyone who challenged them, and still found time to have nine kids together.

Well, I guess it turns out that even though tyranny is fun if you're the tyrant, it didn't really work for the jarls of Norway, and after a couple of years of suffering under Erik and Gunnhild, those guys went looking for help. They found Haakon the Good, the young boy Gunnhild had sent away to be raised by King Athelstan of England (the grandson of Alfred the Great), and asked him if he wanted to be king of Norway. Haakon said sure, returned to Norway with a sword named Quernbiter (because it was so sharp it could cut through a quern, or grinding stone) and a loyal group of followers, and Erik's now bitter jarls and soldiers deserted him almost immediately. Erik Bloodaxe fought Haakon the Good in battle, was defeated, and had to flee Norway.

Queen Gunnhild, driven from her palace by traitors, seethed with rage. She would get her revenge. She swore it.

Gunnhild and Erik Bloodaxe went to England, where they settled in York, the Viking-controlled city that had been captured from the English by Ivar the Boneless. Gunnhild helped establish Erik as the Viking king of York, where he ruled for the next decade or so, issued coins, and spent his summers leading military campaigns to ravage the English, Scottish, and Irish countrysides for goods and supplies. When the people of York threw him out and put some other guy on the throne, Gunnhild and Erik regrouped, attacked, and recaptured the kingdom.

It was a dark day in 954 when word came to Gunnhild that her beloved husband, Erik Bloodaxe, had been killed in battle with the English, and the armies of England were marching toward York. The queen gathered her children, commissioned a boat, and headed to the Orkney Islands, a small group of islands off the coast of Scotland, where her daughter lived with her husband, a powerful jarl named

Thorfinn Skull-Cleaver. Thorfinn took Gunnhild in, and she immediately began strategizing her next move.

From this point on, Gunnhild, Mother of Kings, became even more intense. First, she organized treaties and alliances between Thorfinn and powerful jarls in both England and Norway. She encouraged bands of adventure-hungry Viking raiders to launch attacks up and down the coast of Norway to destabilize Haakon the Good's rule, promising the pirates rewards if she ever regained the throne. She reached out to her brother, King Harald Bluetooth of Denmark, for reinforcements and support. She trained her son, Harald Greycloak, in the arts of leadership and strategy.

After biding her time for seven long years, Gunnhild was ready to make her move.

She arrived off the coast of Norway at the head of a gigantic fleet of warriors from every walk of Viking life—Thorfinn Skull-Cleaver's Orkney men, jarls from York, Danish troops on loan from Harald Bluetooth, and mercenary Viking pirates she'd contacted on remote islands, all unified in one invading armada. When they landed, they were joined by Norwegian forces who had been loyal to Erik or had been promised money and power in the new reign of Gunnhild.

When King Haakon the Good of Norway met Harald Greycloak on the field of battle in 961, Haakon was outnumbered six to one. He fought hard, and bravely, but it wasn't enough. The battle turned, and Haakon was killed—not just

by an arrow, but by Gunnhild's dark magic, if you want to believe the legends.

The real force behind the throne of King Harald Greycloak was Queen Gunnhild, Mother of Kings, who ruled Norway as a tyrant for nine dark years. Land and wealth were seized from disloyal jarls, military raids were launched against would-be usurpers, and all who opposed her were wiped out with extreme brutality.

As you can imagine, this sort of thing doesn't last forever, and Gunnhild, Mother of Kings, was deposed yet again in 970, when another guy named Haakon got mad and raised an army to fight Gunnhild after she set his dad on fire. Supported by the oppressed nobles of Norway, Haakon took his forces into battle with Harald Greycloak, defeated him, and killed the king, and Gunnhild was forced to flee to the Orkneys once again.

Gunnhild went back to work trying to reclaim her throne, but another invasion by her other sons in 971 was defeated by Jarl Haakon. Haakon, not interested in keeping Gunnhild around to thwart him at every turn, made a deal with Harald Bluetooth of Denmark, and Harald sold out his own sister to secure a sweet treaty with Haakon. When Gunnhild returned to Denmark in 974, Harald had his now elderly sister arrested, and sentenced her to death by drowning in a bog.

ᛉ   ᛉ   ᛉ

THE HARALDSKÆR WOMAN

In 1835, the mummified body of a woman floated to the top of a bog in Jutland, Denmark, and was recovered by local villagers. King Frederick VI of Denmark, believing this to be the body of Gunnhild, ordered that an elaborate, expensive sarcophagus be constructed, and had the body laid to rest in a place of honor in a nearby church. Later, radiocarbon dating indicated that this woman had died around 400 BC and wasn't actually Gunnhild. Interestingly, the really nice glass-and-wood casket helped preserve the body incredibly well despite its age, and it remains one of the best examples of an intact body from ancient times.

CALL ME MR. BLOODAXE

Erik Bloodaxe's nickname doesn't just come from his weapon's being almost always completely soaked in blood—the name was given to him because he took an axe to his own family blood-line, coldheartedly killing his half brothers during his grab for power.

AUD THE DEEP-MINDED

An equally cunning but considerably less evil woman from Norse history was Aud the Deep-Minded, a clever Viking noblewoman who saved her family from ultimate destruction. The daughter of powerful *hersir* warriors, Aud married Olaf the White, king of Dublin, in the tenth century. When Olaf was killed in battle with the Irish, Aud fled to Scotland with her son Thorstein the Red. Thorstein became a jarl in Scotland, but just as it looked like things were going to be okay, Thorstein was betrayed and murdered by his own bodyguards. When Aud the Deep-Minded heard the news, she took twenty loyal men and a couple of her slaves and fled into the woods, where she organized the construction of a tricked-out Viking longship. Once that was done, she set sail for Iceland. Commanding the voyage across the treacherous sea, Aud the Deep-Minded got her crew there safely. Once she reached land, she immediately freed her slaves, claimed a large tract of land for herself, and got to work building a nice quiet farm where she would spend the rest of her days. Some historians claim that Aud and Olaf were actually Ota and Turgeis the Devil, our friends who plundered Ireland in chapter 3, but this probably isn't the case.

VİKİNG WARRİOR WOMEN

> There were once women in Denmark who dressed themselves to look like men [and] sought the clash of arms rather than the arms' embrace.
>
> —Saxo Grammaticus, *The Danish History*

The early history of Denmark is shrouded in mystery and mythology, available to us only through a few unfortunately unreliable sources, but in these early days there are plenty of stories of ultra-intense warrior women who charged screaming into battle, spears, axes, and swords at the ready, seeking either to achieve bloody glory or to die horribly in the process. While few if any of these stories can be verified by trustworthy sources, here are some of the great warrior women from Danish history.

The Shield-Maidens

At the Battle of Bravalla, a legendary battle that probably took place in the early 700s, the Danish king Harald Wartooth (which is *such* an awesome name) took a massive army into battle against a rival king in one of the largest engagements of pre-Viking Scandinavian history. According to the epic, presumably embellished story,

which is basically the Viking version of the *Iliad* or the *Mahabharata* (look them up!), the heart of Wartooth's formation featured a unit of three hundred warrior women known as the shield-maidens. Equipped with long swords and round shields, the shield-maidens were led by a ferocious warrior woman named Wisna, who had one of her hands cut off during the fighting. In the mass destruction and mayhem that ensued, one of her fellow warriors, Veborg, cut a guy's jaw off and hung his beard from her armor, and then took out a guy named Thorkell the Stubborn "after much arguing." Shield-maidens, however, weren't limited to this battle. When the Vikings of Russia attacked Constantinople in the early 900s, the Byzantine Empire's chroniclers were

horrified to report that armored women were found among
the ranks of the Viking dead.

Pirates and Raiders

If marriage, home life, and raising kids weren't your
thing, a Viking girl in the 800s could always try piracy.
The Norse warrior woman Stikla went pirate to avoid marriage, as did the Swedish noblewoman Alfhild, both of them
choosing to don armor and sail the high seas, plundering
and raiding as a way of making ends meet. Alfhild actually commanded a crew of bloodthirsty pirate women she'd
recruited from England, Germany, and the Viking lands.
Rusila, a daughter of a *hersir*, recruited a band of marauders to help her fight her brother for control of the family's
estate, and when that didn't work, she just declared war
on Denmark as a whole and launched countless attacks up
and down the coast. Described by the historian Saxo as
having "bodies of women and souls of men," these Viking
sea-queens ravaged the waterways of the North Sea with
impunity, plundering and pillaging all they could find.

Lagertha

A Norwegian noblewoman who did battle with the invading Swedes in the early ninth century, Lagertha charged
into battle dressed as a man, and stood out on the battlefield
because of the long hair coming out the back of her helmet.

Her bravery in combat thoroughly impressed semi-legendary Viking hero Ragnar Hairy-Breeches, and the two even ended up being married for a short time. Lagertha became a raider and a pirate, eventually married a powerful jarl, then killed the guy in an argument and seized control of his kingdom.

Hervor

At a time when other girls in her village were learning how to knit and weave and paint pots and do other boring nonsense, the Viking shield-maiden Hervor was practicing horsemanship, archery, and sword fighting, routinely beating the neighbor boys into crumpled heaps or sending them running home to their mommies with black eyes and broken bones. She turned Viking and won honor with her father's blade, the supposedly dwarf-forged sword Tyrfing, a weapon that had a hilt fashioned of solid gold and was so deadly that just a nick from the blade was universally fatal. However, Tyrfing was also cursed, and every time it was drawn from its scabbard, it consumed a life—sometimes by driving the wielder insane and forcing him to slaughter one of his own friends. Hervor was a scourge of the countryside for many years, but eventually she settled down, had some kids, and raised them to be heroes. Her largely mythological story (she has to talk to ghosts to get the sword) served as an inspiration for the character Eowyn in Tolkien's *Lord of the Rings* trilogy.

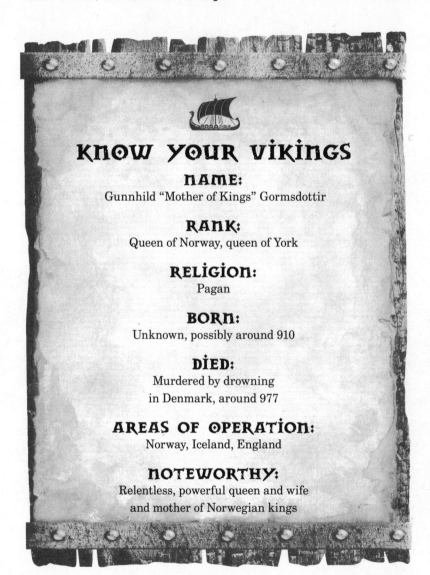

KNOW YOUR VIKINGS

NAME:
Gunnhild "Mother of Kings" Gormsdottir

RANK:
Queen of Norway, queen of York

RELIGION:
Pagan

BORN:
Unknown, possibly around 910

DIED:
Murdered by drowning
in Denmark, around 977

AREAS OF OPERATION:
Norway, Iceland, England

NOTEWORTHY:
Relentless, powerful queen and wife
and mother of Norwegian kings

THE SIEGE OF PARIS

Vikings at the gates of the City of Love
October AD 885–spring AD 886

On every side arrows sped and blood flowed. With the arrows mingled the stones hurled by slings and war-machines; the air was filled with them. The tower which had been built during the night groaned under the strokes of the darts, the city shook with the struggle, the people ran hither and thither, the bells jangled. The warriors rushed together to defend the tottering tower and repel the fierce assault. Among these warriors two, a count and an abbot, surpassed all the rest in courage.

—Abbo de Saint-Germain, *De Bellis Parisiacae*

N THE MORNING OF NOVEMBER 25, 885, a dreadful sight approached on the distant horizon. Making its way up the Seine River, straight for the heart of Paris, was the largest Viking armada anyone had ever seen. Seven hundred black dragon-headed Viking longships, carrying a host of over thirty thousand bloodthirsty warriors, aligned in a battle formation that stretched over seven miles downriver. Their red-and-white sails flying high, their crews of sweaty oarsmen rowing with all their might, the Vikings raced ahead, eager to capture the jewel of the Frankish Empire. Victory would grant them access to a crossroads of three mighty rivers, giving the largest Viking fleet in French history unrestricted access to waterways throughout the countryside.

The small Frankish garrison, probably not numbering more than a few hundred men, sealed the gates, strapped on their armor, and called for their leader, the fearless Count Odo Capet. Son of Duke Robert the Strong, Odo was a valiant knight, a resolute fighter, and the man entrusted with the safety of his beloved city. Within the walls were tens of thousands of loyal subjects, not the least of whom were his own wife and infant son, and he was determined to protect them from the Viking scourge at all costs.

The leader of the Viking flotilla, a humorless, gigantic sea-king named Sigfried, called to Count Odo to meet and discuss terms. Sigfried and a few of his jarls met with Count Odo and Joscelyn, the bishop of Paris, on neutral ground, and Sigfried made his demand: "You open the path for us to travel down the Seine, and we promise we totally won't double-cross you and sack Paris. You have my word as a bloodthirsty, utterly untrustworthy Viking marauder who wants nothing more than to chop off your head and decorate my living room with it."

Bishop Joscelyn and Count Odo didn't trust this guy as far as they could throw a refrigerator full of Norsemen. The clergyman responded by saying, "If, like us, you had been given the duty of defending these walls, and if you should have done that which you ask us to do, what treatment do you think you would deserve?"

Sigfried put his fists down on the table and stared the bishop in the eyes. His response: "I should deserve that my head be cut off and thrown to the dogs. Nevertheless, if you do not listen to my demand, on the morrow our war machines will destroy you with poisoned arrows. You will be the prey of famine and of pestilence and those evils will renew themselves perpetually every year."

Then he calmly stood, turned, and left, followed closely by his grim companions.

It was about to get real.

Paris was defended by two sets of impressive Viking-proof stone walls that clamped the city up tighter than a fallout shelter. The first wall surrounded the city itself, and the second was a fortified bridge outside town, bristling with arrow loops and turrets that barred access to the Seine. Odo's men had closed the bridge defenses in time, but throughout the rest of November 25, the Vikings unloaded their ships, started putting together their catapults, dusted off their battle gear, and prepared to take the bridge by force. The count ordered his men to gather any and all weapons and equipment they could find from the town, take up positions in the tower on the bridge, and prepare for the fight of their lives.

Sigfried launched his attack at dawn the next morning with an aerial barrage of catapult stones that hammered into the bridge tower and wall like giant wrecking balls. Each massive boulder was launched out of a catapult the size of a city bus. The defenders, firing out through arrow slits in the tower, tried to take down the catapults, but the sea of warriors in front of them was honestly pretty terrifying (Helm's Deep kind of stuff). Count Odo and Bishop Joscelyn did the best they could to keep morale up, with the armored count racing up and down the lines shouting pump-up speeches and the bishop offering prayers for the protection of the men and constantly reminding them to fight for God against the heathen enemies.

After softening up the defenses, Sigfried ordered an all-out assault. Teams of Viking warriors raced forward, some of them carrying super-tall ladders and others holding their shields over their heads to deflect the incoming arrows and crossbow bolts raining down on them from the Frankish men-at-arms. The warriors threw the ladders up on the walls, trying to scale the tower, but every time, the defenders threw them back, with Count Odo himself personally dumping pots of scalding-hot oil, boiling water, and burning pitch down on their heads. The Vikings, driven back by a storm of arrows and molten liquid, ran for their lives or jumped into the river to put out the fires, but the damage done to the tower during the day was catastrophic. It was clear the Parisians would not hold for long.

That night, Count Odo and Bishop Joscelyn ran through the streets of Paris, rallying the citizens to their aid. Teams of Parisian men and women ran to the walls, working from dusk to dawn to repair the damage done by the Vikings during the day, while the exhausted warriors rested and tended to their wounds.

When the Vikings awoke the following morning, not only was the bridge tower as good as new, but the Parisians had added another level to it during the night, making it that much tougher to climb and that much easier to defend.

The none-too-discouraged Vikings attempted a second attack, trying to break through the bridge by setting fire to their own boats and crashing them into the mighty gate that crossed the river, but still the defenses held. As eight-hundred-pound catapult and trebuchet boulders rained overhead, Viking teams carrying a huge iron-plated battering

ram tried to force the gates to the tower, but once again the count and his men repulsed them, this time by racing to the breaches in the wall and fighting the Vikings off face-to-face. At one point, a Paris ballista (basically, a truck-sized cross-bow) fired a huge arrow into the breach. It impaled seven Vikings in a single shot as they all tried to climb through a small hole in the wall.

Thrown back twice, with heavy casualties, the Vikings decided, "Hey, maybe we should stop running at the arrows and burning oil and just lay siege to the city." They sur-rounded Paris, cut off access to the roads, and settled in to starve the population into submission. For two months the Vikings waited, letting supply shortages and disease eat away at the battered defenders. Even worse, nasty flooding in January caused the bridge to fail, breaking open access to the Seine and forcing the Parisian defenders to fall back to the city walls. The Vikings tried one more attack on the city itself but were again thrown back by crossbows, arrows, and civilians pitching everything from rocks to household items down from the walls onto the approaching Danes.

The Vikings maintained the siege for another six months but still could not get the stubborn people of Paris to just open the stupid doors and let them come in and murder every-one. The Vikings tried filling in the moat with straw, dead animals, and lumber, but every night the Parisians threw the junk out of there. The invaders tried digging tunnels underneath the city, hoping to bring down the walls, but that didn't work, either.

While all this was going on, people from both sides started flocking to Paris to get in on the action. A few Frankish noblemen launched attacks to try to drive the Vikings off, none of which were successful, and while some Vikings (including Sigfried himself) got bored and went home, many more showed up to reinforce their ranks. With the food supply of the city rapidly going away, and terrible living conditions bringing about a host of killer diseases like malaria and rubella that decimated the population, Count Odo Capet knew that the only way to end this was with the help of the emperor himself.

He resolved to make a break for it and personally demand that the emperor come to the aid of his people.

In the middle of the night, Count Odo Capet left his wife, son, and troops and snuck past the Viking siege lines with a small group of elite bodyguard knights. He rode for the imperial palace of Charles the Fat, stopping along the way to tell every knight and noble he could find that Paris needed his help.

Meanwhile, back in the city, Bishop Joscelyn fell ill and died of the plague that was racking the town. The Parisians, their leaders gone, started to think the end was near.

Then, on a faraway hill, they saw the sun glinting off the

armor of a small band of Frankish knights. It was Count Odo Capet, returning to town, completely unafraid to try to cleave his way through the entire Viking army and return to his people. A huge cheer went up from the city.

The Vikings tried to block Count Odo's way, but he formed his knights into a wedge and smashed into the Viking lines, cutting down enemy warriors left and right and clearing a path to the city gates. His men opened the doors for Odo and his bodyguard, then slammed them shut just before the Vikings could get close. Odo called the people together and told them to have hope—the emperor was coming for them. Just hold on a little bit longer.

The people would have to suffer through a few more months of starvation, disease, and constant hammering from

Viking siege weaponry and arrows. Finally, late in October 866, after over a year of waiting, the imperial army finally approached, led by Charles the Fat himself.

Except Charles hadn't come to sweep the enemy from the field and liberate Paris from her oppressors. He'd come to negotiate like a wimp.

He told the Vikings they could have seven hundred pounds of silver and free access to the Seine River, but only if they left Paris alone and promised to plunder only Charles's enemies in the neighboring kingdom of Burgundy.

Naturally, the Vikings agreed.

If it kind of seems to you like Charles the Fat was selling out his own people just to avoid having to fight the Vikings, you're not alone. The French nobles, livid about his inept and bumbling handling of the situation, declared Emperor Charles the Fat unfit to rule in 888, stripped him of his crown, and then told a bunch of mean jokes making fun of his weight. In his place, they crowned none other than the heroic Count Odo Capet, the defender of Paris. Odo assumed the throne, assembled the imperial army, and went to work getting those Vikings the heck out of his country. He took the fight to them, engaged them at the Battle of Montfaucon in 888, and personally led the attack. In the ensuing battle, King Odo took a battle-axe blow that clanged off his helmet, but he recovered in time to kill the enemy general with a sword to the heart and drive his shattered army from the field. King Odo gave the Viking band he had faced at Paris one condition to end the fighting: "I'll honor Charles the Fat's word to pay you what we owe you, but you are to leave and never return."

They did.

The people of the Frankish Kingdom hadn't heard the last of the Viking armadas that had ravaged their lands for the past fifty years, but it was certainly a step in the right direction. The beginning of the end was in sight.

THE CAPETIANS

As tough and dedicated as King Odo Capet was, years of incompetence by previous rulers meant that he simply didn't have the infrastructure, money, or manpower to defeat Viking raiding parties everywhere in his kingdom. Viking raids continued, Odo faced challenges to his rule across the kingdom, and the new king had to choose his battles carefully. Odo ruled from 888 to 898 but was eventually replaced by the legitimate-by-birth successor to Charles the Fat, Charles the Simple. France hadn't heard the last of Count Odo, however; his descendants would reclaim the throne and establish the Capetian Dynasty, which would rule France for more than 350 years.

CHARLESES in CHARGE

Keeping track of all the Carolingian Frankish kings from this time is kind of a pain, mostly because they're all named Charles, Louis, or Pippin. Even if you don't include pre-Viking Frankish king Charlemagne (which means "Charles the Great") and Charles Martel (meaning "Charles the Hammer"), you've still got Charles the Fat, Charles the Simple, Charles the Bald, Charles the Younger, and Charles the Child, as well as Louis the Pious, Louis II, Louis the German, Louis the Younger, Louis the Stammerer, Pippin the Short, Pippin the Hunchback, and Pippin of Italy.

CHARLES THE FAT

During his reign, nobody had the guts to refer to the emperor as "Charles the Fat," and the chubster nickname didn't really start appearing until about three hundred years after Chuck was dead. Today, we aren't even sure if he was actually fat or not. But it's probably a safe bet that he was.

Know Your Viking History

Name:
Count Odo Capet

Rank:
Count of Anjou,
king of Western Francia

Religion:
Catholic

Born:
Western France, around 850

Died:
La Fère, France, January 1, 898

Area of Operation:
France

Noteworthy:
Daring Frankish knight who heroically
saved Paris from a vicious Viking attack

HROLF
THE WALKER

A homeless sea-raider becomes
an iron-fisted Frankish count
AD 846–931

The number of ships increases, the endless flood of Vikings never ceases to grow bigger. Everywhere Christ's people are the victims of massacre, burning and plunder. The Vikings overrun all that lies before them, and none can withstand them.

—Ermentarius, Frankish scholar

S WE'VE JUST SEEN, THE KINGS OF THE Franks in the late ninth century were almost all completely worthless, and their bumbling idiocy had already done a fairly tremendous job of successfully transforming the once-mighty empire of Charlemagne into a Viking-ravaged wasteland of human existence. Bloody succession disputes between pointless wannabe kings, a crippled economy, relentless Viking attacks, and the complete inability to do anything inside their own borders doomed the descendants of the Great Emperor. By the year 900, crime and lawlessness were so over-the-top ridiculous that kings had been reduced to making their counts and dukes sign paperwork promising not to rob their own citizens and burn their own cities down on a whim. Town guards were given instructions to dish out the law "as best you can remember." Bandits roamed the countryside. Vikings controlled the coastal waterways. Entire cities lay in ruins, monasteries had been stripped bare, and once-opulent cathedrals now stood empty, their bishops dead, enslaved, or fleeing for their lives.

Nearly all of northern France had been reduced to a lawless sprawl of burned-out misery. And aside from the short reign of Odo, the kings of the Franks did nothing.

We're not sure exactly where the Viking warrior Hrolf came from. In fact, in another example of the sort of thing that makes most medieval historians want to dig their eyes out with a grapefruit spoon, we're not even sure what this guy's name was—we're pretty certain it was *definitely* either Rollo, Rollon, Rodulf, Ruinus, Rosso, Rotlo, Rolf, Hrolf, Robert, Bob, Rob, or Bobby. Probably. One story claims that he was the son of a prominent Danish nobleman who had been banished from the land by the king of Denmark because he was too popular and was a potential threat to the king's rule. A second, completely different story claims that Hrolf was a Norwegian who had raided the coasts of Norway during Harold Fairhair's reign and had been outlawed despite the best efforts of his mom, who threw herself on Fairhair's mercy and begged for her son's life.

Either way, if we play the odds, we know that Hrolf (I settled on Hrolf only because it sounds the most Viking-y) was a Northman and that he was probably banished from his homeland by his king. There are also a couple of sagas that refer to him as Ganger Rolf, or Hrolf the Walker, because this gigantor Norse face-smasher was so over-the-top huge that he had to walk around everywhere, since no horse could carry him. And, let's face it here, being the Shaq of Vikings is pretty amazing.

When you're talking about a Viking massive enough to snap a horse in half with his body, you know that Hrolf the Walker was a pretty righteous warrior. No pitchfork-swinging peasant in his right mind would ever want to do anything except run screaming from a guy this size wielding a two-handed Danish long axe that was probably as big as a telephone pole. After his exile from home, Hrolf proved his might as a Viking raider time and time again, pillaging and plundering mostly along the already ravaged northern coast of present-day France. He might have been a minor lieutenant at the Siege of Paris in 885 (probably not), but by 895 he had been elected by his men to command the Vikings who had hung around after the rest of the Paris crew had headed home.

Fighting in Burgundy and northern Frankland, Hrolf became famous for his cunning, leadership, and bench-pressing ability. A good example of this is when he captured the still-impressive walled city of Rouen with just fifteen ships. He parked his ships on the banks of the river, dug a bunch of huge pitholes, covered them with turf, and then stormed the imposing city walls with just a few hundred men. When the Frankish heavy cavalry came out to skewer the Viking intruders on the points of their lances, Hrolf and his men ran for it, leading the knights right into their trap. The knights fell into the holes and got stuck, and the Vikings laughed hysterically as they walked right in the front door (the knights had left it unlocked). Then, in 911, Hrolf marched on and laid siege to Chartres, a wealthy city just sixty miles from Paris.

The new Frankish king, Charles the Simple, had finally had enough. He met with Hrolf the Walker and said, "Okay, here's the deal—this area has been too often laid waste by Hasting and you, so why don't we do this: You marry my daughter Gisla, the princess of the Franks, and I give you a

ton of territory on the coast that you Vikings have been pillaging so hard. In return, you convert to Christianity, swear
allegiance to me, and rule as one of my counts."

This sounded pretty good to Hrolf the Walker. It wasn't
like he had a home to go to, anyway. He agreed.

To seal the deal, Charles the Simple stepped forward and
demanded a humiliating show of loyalty that the Frankish
kings traditionally received from every knight who swore
allegiance to them: Hrolf the Walker had to kneel down and
kiss Charles the Simple's toe ring.

This part of the deal didn't work for the gigantic Viking.
He narrowed his eyes, clenched his teeth, and told the king
of the Franks, "I will never bow my knees at the knees of any
man, and no man's foot will I kiss."

Then Hrolf ordered one of his warriors to do the deed
for him. Hrolf's big, scary Viking bodyguard walked over
to Charles, and instead of kneeling to kiss the ring, the
dude grabbed the king's leg, pulled the toe ring up to his
mouth, kissed it, and then pushed Charles over onto his
back.

The Vikings all laughed their butts off. But the deal was
done, and Hrolf the Walker, Viking marauder, was now
Robert I, Count of Rouen. His land, a big chunk of coastline in present-day France, became known as the *Terra
Normannorum*, "Land of the Norsemen."

Nowadays we call the region Normandy.

Despite living the life of an outlaw up to this point, Count Robert took his job very, very seriously. His first task was to clean up this area that he and his buddies had just ravaged into charred cinders. He rebuilt towns. He erected huge, impenetrable walls around important cities. He constructed fortresses overlooking coastal waterways and organized a militia to deal with raiders. He sent his Viking warriors to wipe out bandit gangs and highwaymen, and to clean up the roads and forests of punks, evil-doers, brigands, and other dastardly fellows. He also went to work cracking down on crime, ordering that offenses like robbery and assault were to be punished by summary execution.

Diligent, hardworking, and iron-fisted in his rule, Count Robert adapted his Viking-style sense of vengeance to every aspect of his government. Once, a man and his wife hid some of their farming tools and then accused their neighbor of stealing the stuff. When the truth came out, Robert had the man and his wife beaten, hanged for a few minutes, then cut down and "finished off by a cruel death." Another time, a man looked at Robert's wife funny, so Robert had that guy and his friends tortured to death with red-hot irons.

Count Robert's wrath terrified the population of Normandy, but it worked. Before long, crime was wiped out, bandit gangs had been eradicated, and churches and towns were bustling with people flocking not only from Frankland but also from Denmark and Norway. Viking raids on the Seine ended, and any Northman dumb enough to test Count Robert found himself facing an enemy who not only knew all their tricks but had already done them better.

Once his borders were secure, Count Robert expanded the land of Normandy through treaties with other Frankish nobles as well as through military campaigns that destroyed rivals along the northern coast of France.

At the time of his death in 931, Hrolf the Walker had gone from a little-known but gigantic Viking pillager to the Count of Normandy. His heirs, descending from his son, William Longsword, would eventually be upgraded from Counts of Rouen to Dukes of Normandy and would become more and more integrated with Frankish (and later French) society.

The most famous of these descendants was Hrolf's great-great-great grandson, a man known as William the Conqueror, who would lead a mighty, history-changing invasion of the British Isles in 1066 that would end with his being crowned King William I of England.

But that's a tale for a different chapter. (Check out chapter 20 if you just can't wait.)

GODFRID'S RAID

In 882, a particularly ambitious Danish king named Godfrid marched into the heart of Charlemagne's once-mighty empire, burning monasteries and towns along the way. Godfrid even pushed as far as Charlemagne's old capital at Aachen, stripping the emperor's palace of its riches and then letting his horses sleep inside it for the night. Charles the Fat marched with an army to meet Godfrid, but instead of going to war, Charles offered Godfrid a bunch of money, an imperial princess, and a dukedom in Frisia to go away. Godfrid snatched it up but was assassinated three years later, probably on Charles's orders.

ALAIN TWISTED-BEARD

Hrolf the Walker effectively made Normandy a no-trespass zone for Vikings, so they headed west to work their magic on the region of Brittany, located at the northwestern tip of present-day France. The guy in charge there, a Frankish noble named Alain Barbetorte (meaning "twisted beard"), was overrun by the onslaught, but he regrouped, got together his best knights, and in 936 crashed a Viking wedding where he killed everyone involved and then possibly twirled his mustache evilly. Barbetorte beat the Vikings again and again, retaking his region from the invaders. Things were pretty cool for him until a few years later, when one of Hrolf's descendants came in with a big army and told everyone that Brittany was part of Normandy now.

KNOW YOUR VIKINGS

NAME:
Hrolf "the Walker"

RANK:
Count of Rouen

RELIGION:
Catholic (converted 911)

BORN:
Unknown, probably Denmark, around 846

DIED:
Natural causes, Normandy, 931

AREA OF OPERATION:
France

NOTEWORTHY:
Was appointed Count of Rouen
by the king of the Franks, who wanted to stop him
from ravaging the countryside

EGIL
SKALLAGRIMSSON

Battle-raging berserker, world-renowned poet
c. AD 910–990

With bloody brand on-striding
My bird of bane hath followed;
My hurtling spear hath sounded
In the swift Vikings' charge.
Raged wrathfully our battle,
Ran fire o'er foemen's rooftrees;
Sound sleepeth many a warrior
Slain in the city gate.

—Egil's Saga

EGIL SKALLAGRIMSSON WAS AN UTTERLY
unstoppable Viking warrior and skald unmatched
in physical strength, skill in combat, and eloquence
of verse. He spent his life sailing the seas, plundering towns,

slaying his enemies, and having the sorts of adventures that would make him one of the most famous antiheroes in Viking history. He did battle with armies of mighty warriors, cut his enemies apart with an axe, and once killed a wolf with his bare hands and ate it raw.

Oh, right, and he also wrote two of the most famous poems in the history of medieval Iceland and is believed to be one of the best literary minds of the Viking Age.

Wait, what?

As his name would suggest, Egil was the son of a man named Skallagrim, who was a prominent landowner and nobleman in Norway. Things started getting hairy for Skallagrim when King Harald Fairhair was doing his "conquer all of Norway" thing, so he left and set up shop in Iceland, where Egil and his older brother, Thorolf, were born. Egil was strong, talkative, clever, and incredibly grouchy. His large body, broad shoulders, and thick neck were made all the more imposing by the fact that he had a large, weirdly shaped head that kind of looked like an eggplant with eyes. It's described as being one of the ugliest heads ever seen in Viking history, and his skull was allegedly so thick in some places that it once deflected an axe blow. That, coupled with his horrible temper, has led some modern doctors to believe he suffered from Paget's disease, an incredibly painful disorder in which the bones continually change shape. Egil did not have a sense of humor about this.

Egil first started showing signs of his sunny personal-
ity at the tender age of seven, when he was out on the play-
ground and some neighborhood bully beat him up. Rather
than run home and cry about it, Egil handled the situation
like a Viking: He picked up a nearby axe and dropped the
bully with one swing, setting off a family feud that ended up
killing half a dozen people. Survey says: Don't mess with Egil
Skallagrimsson.

At the age of fourteen, Egil did what any respectable
tenth-century Icelandic man worth his bearskins would do:
He joined up with a Viking raiding party. One of their first
destinations was a nearby island where a dude named Bard—
who was a good friend and servant of King Erik Bloodaxe
of Norway—put them up. Egil, who had a little too much to
drink (there is a reason the most popular beer in Iceland is
named after him), believed Bard was trying to poison him, so
he stabbed his host in the middle of the dinner hall, fled into
the woods to avoid being arrested for murder, swam through
a freezing-cold harbor, climbed onto a boat, killed the Vikings
on board, and rowed out of there by himself. He spent the rest
of his life evading the long arm of the law, with Erik Bloodaxe
and his wife, Gunnhild, constantly sending people to murder
or arrest him.

Here's a tip: It's not good to make an enemy of a Viking
king named Bloodaxe. And we've already seen what Queen
Gunnhild Kingsmother was capable of.

The next summer, Egil headed out with his brother, Thorolf, and they sailed up and down the European coastline, sacking cities and plundering merchant vessels. At one point, while in the kingdom of Courland (in present-day Lithuania), Egil and his men were ambushed by a large force and imprisoned in a dungeon. Egil's hands and feet were bound to a large pole, and his captors informed him that he and his men would

all be tortured to death the following day. That night, while the Courlanders were partying and drinking in a large dining hall, Egil managed to break free by wrenching the pole out of the ground and chewing through his bindings. He freed his comrades, broke through the door of his cell, and found the Courlanders' armory. The Vikings looted the armory and the palace's treasury and then stealthily made their way outside with armfuls of gold and silver.

However, Egil didn't feel right about this. He told his companions to wait for him as he headed back inside the palace. Once inside, he barred all the exits from the dining hall except one and then set the place on fire. When his captors called out, "Who is responsible for this!" Egil responded: "Here now is that same Egil whom you bound hand and foot to the post in that room you shut so carefully. I will repay you your hospitality as you deserve!"

The Courlanders lucky enough to escape the fire were cut down by Egil as they came through the door. Everyone else burned to death.

Not long after this, Erik Bloodaxe's wife, Queen Gunnhild, Mother of Kings, sent two of her brothers out to kill Egil and his brother, Thorolf. When Egil heard about this plot, he didn't do what any sensible person would and simply watch his back. He changed course, found Gunnhild's brothers, ambushed their camp, killed every single person he found, burned their ships, and stole all their plunder.

Well, now the Skallagrimsson brothers realized they were in deep trouble in Norway, so they sailed their crew over to England and offered their services to King Athelstan of the Britons. Athelstan, the grandson of Alfred the Great, was in the middle of wars with the Vikings, the Scots, and the Welsh, so he was obviously pretty psyched about having an army of some three hundred Vikings at his disposal, and he let them join up.

A few months later, the Viking king Olaf of Scotland launched an attack on Athelstan's kingdom, and Egil once again tasted battle. While scouting ahead in search of the main enemy force, Egil and Thorolf got embroiled in combat with two Scottish earls, and despite being outnumbered, they were able to defeat the much larger enemy force on the battlefield.

The next morning the main forces of Olaf and Athelstan met in combat. When Thorolf was killed in battle by the Scots, Egil pulled his sword, flew into a blood rage, and charged forward like a berserker. He crashed into the nearest Scottish division, slaughtering an earl, his color guard, and anyone else who crossed him. The earl's unit fell into a full retreat, and Egil's men gave chase, cutting down the routed Scots forces. The Scottish lines subsequently broke, and King Olaf was killed in battle, along with five jarls and a few other minor kings. Though the battle was over, Egil and his men continued pursuing the broken Scottish forces for several days before finally returning to bury Thorolf. Egil would later mention Thorolf in his poem *The Loss of a Son*, a heartbreaking lamentation composed after the death of two of Egil's sons, and a poem now believed to be one of the finest in Icelandic history. You can check it out online on the Guts & Glory website (gutsandgloryhistory.com)!

At the victory banquet, Egil was given two chests full of silver by the king, as well as a bunch of other sweet swag. He returned home to Norway for the winter to mourn his brother and break the news to his brother's wife, Asgerdr. During the winter, Egil and Asgerdr fell in love and were married, which sounds pretty weird today but was kind of common for the time period.

Now, Asgerdr was the daughter of a wealthy landowner in Norway. After the wedding, she and Egil moved back to Iceland to be with Egil's dad for a few years. During that time, Asgerdr's father died, and her brother-in-law snatched up all of what (Egil believed) was her rightful inheritance. So she and Egil headed back to Norway to deal with it. Unfortunately, the brother-in-law was a dude named Bergonund, who was tight with Queen Gunnhild, Egil's mortal enemy. So of course the queen and the royal court sided with Bergonund.

Now, if you've been paying attention to this epic saga so far, Egil Skallagrimsson isn't the kind of guy who's going to sit back when he thinks he's been wronged. First, he sailed out to Bergonund's island and defeated him and two of his bodyguards in hand-to-hand combat. Then he plundered Bergonund's household of all the inheritance he believed belonged to Asgerdr, and placed a curse on the entire ruling family of Norway before finally heading back home to Iceland. A few years later, Bergonund's brother, Atli the Short, made another claim on Asgerdr's inheritance, so Egil dueled with him as well. In the fight, Egil's shield and sword got broken, but he killed Atli by tackling him to the turf and *biting his throat out.*

Over the years, Egil had many other crazy adventures, very few of which can be proven as historical fact. One claims that a feared berserker named Ljot the Pale came to Egil's best friend's nephew and challenged him to a duel he had absolutely no chance of winning. Egil went along to watch the duel, and when Ljot started Hulking up and bit a piece off his wooden shield with his teeth, Egil started singing a song to taunt him. Ljot forgot about the nephew and challenged Egil instead. They dueled, and Egil cut the dude's leg off.

Another tale has him heading through a dense, treacherous, rocky forest where he and his men were ambushed by about fifteen bandits. Egil ran up and hacked eight of them single-handedly in about fifteen seconds, and then he started hurling rocks at the other seven guys, who ran off

and returned with even more of their buddies. In the ensuing battle, Egil was jumped by eleven guys at once and defeated them all at the same time, like something out of a kung fu movie.

King Erik and Queen Gunnhild did eventually catch up with Egil, capturing the Viking warrior when he washed ashore after a shipwreck. Thrown into a dungeon and sentenced to be executed the following morning, Egil flexed another powerful muscle—his mind. He spent the entire night composing a poem called *Head Ransom*, praising Erik and requesting a pardon for his crimes. The poem was so moving that when Egil was done reciting it, Erik gave him a full pardon and let him go free. Gunnhild still thought he should die horribly, but that's Gunnhild for you.

To understand how a guy got off death row with nothing more than a sweet poem and a winning smile, it's important to understand that to the Vikings, poetry, writing, runes, and story crafting were all considered gifts from Odin himself. These arts were thought to be highly magical, brought to the world from Valhalla itself, and people who were talented in them were favorites of Odin. So when Egil publicly recited a poem describing the king's numerous heroic deeds, Erik realized he was being immortalized not only in verse but with the gods themselves. The king did not forgive Egil for his crimes, but he did grudgingly release him.

After his many years of adventuring, fighting, and singing, Egil returned to Iceland to raise his four children, share his wisdom with travelers, heal the sick, and settle occasional disputes. He accumulated massive amounts of wealth and property, owned a huge, successful farm in Iceland, and lived like royalty until he died of illness at the age of eighty.

Today, more than for his sword arm, Egil Skallagrimsson is remembered as one of the most eloquent poets of the Viking Age.

Once with eight I battled
Eleven faced I twice,
Made for wolf a meal,
Myself the bane of all.
Shields shook by sword-strokes
Smitten fast and furious;
Angry fire forth-flashing
Flew my ashen spear.

I LIKED THE ORIGINAL BETTER

Although an army of teachers consider it the greatest work of fiction ever written, Shakespeare's *Hamlet* was actually based on a Danish legend written down by historian Saxo Grammaticus in the twelfth century, about three hundred years before Shakespeare penned the remake.

TRIAL BY COMBAT

The holmgang was a Viking duel fought to avenge one's honor against a hated adversary. Two warriors would get together, draw a big circle, and then duke it out inside the circle with swords and shields until someone either gave up or died. One foot stepping out of the circle counted as yielding (surrendering honorably), and two feet out counted as running away. Fleeing, declining a challenge to a duel, and peeing your pants in the middle of a fight were all considered acts of ultimate cowardice.

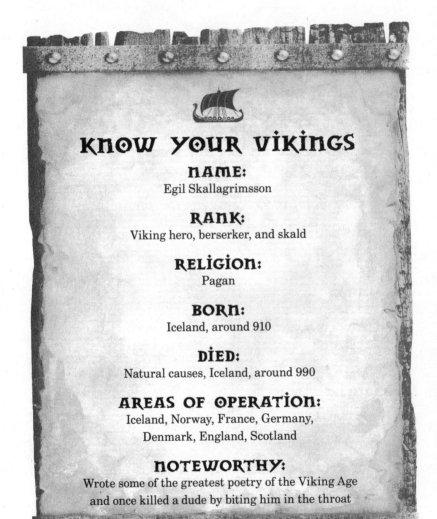

Know your vikings

Name:
Egil Skallagrimsson

Rank:
Viking hero, berserker, and skald

Religion:
Pagan

Born:
Iceland, around 910

Died:
Natural causes, Iceland, around 990

Areas of operation:
Iceland, Norway, France, Germany,
Denmark, England, Scotland

Noteworthy:
Wrote some of the greatest poetry of the Viking Age
and once killed a dude by biting him in the throat

SAINT OLGA OF KIEV

Vengeful Viking warrior-princess
turned Russian Orthodox saint
AD 890–969

> When the Derevlians arrived, Olga commanded that a bath should be made ready, and invited them to appear before her after they had bathed. The bathhouse was then heated, and the Derevlians entered in to bathe. Olga's men closed up the bathhouse behind them, and she gave orders to set it on fire from the doors, so that the Derevlians were all burned to death.
>
> —*The Russian Primary Chronicle*

SAINT OLGA OF KIEV WAS A VIKING WARRIOR-princess who unleashed a dump truck of bloody vengeance on all who opposed her, cleansed the countryside of her enemies in a sea of unquenchable flames, conquered hordes of vicious barbarians, and saved her people during the Siege of Kiev with nothing more than her own fearlessness. She also instituted the first taxation system in Eastern Europe, built the first stone structures in Russia, and once buried twenty foreign dignitaries alive. And she somehow still managed to be sainted by the Orthodox Church for almost single-handedly turning Russia into a Christian country.

Born in Pskov, Russia, around 890, Olga was the daughter of powerful Swedish aristocrats who had moved to Russia not long after Rurik had taken over the show there. Known in Old Norse as Helga (the Russians pronounced it "Olga" because that sounded much more Russian to them), this tough-as-nails lady married Rurik's son, Prince Igor of Novgorod, in 903. When Igor's uncle (who had been named regent to rule for the young prince until he was old enough to do it himself) died in 912, Igor took over as ruler of Kievan Rus, and Olga found herself the powerful princess of an empire that spanned parts of modern-day Russia, Ukraine, Belarus, and Poland.

Igor did some killing and conquering-type stuff around Kiev and Novgorod, but things turned bad for him in 945, when he got a little too greedy and tried to demand that a Slavic tribe known as the Drevlyans pay him money to not attack them. According to the ancient chronicles, Igor rode into enemy territory with a few of his buddies and told the Drevlyans he was coming to steal all the silver in their empire. King Mal of Drevlya responded by ambushing Prince Igor, slaughtering his honor guard, decapitating him, and turning his skull into a decorative wine goblet he could show off at dinner parties. No, seriously, he actually did this.

In his mind, little King Mal of Drevlya (king of a tiny tribe nobody outside Russia had ever heard of) had won a great victory against the Vikings, saved his civilization from paying an unreasonable tribute demanded by an enemy tyrant, and vanquished the prince of Kiev once and for all.

Then Mal pushed his luck. He sent a team of twenty ambassadors to Kiev for two reasons—first, to inform Princess Olga that her husband had met an untimely sword-related demise, and second, to demand her hand in marriage. Together, he reasoned, they could unite the kingdoms of Kiev and Drevlya into one powerful Viking-Slavic empire.

I'll give you two guesses how this one went over with Olga, a born-and-bred Viking warrior woman who only really had a sense of humor when it came to things like burning people to death or throwing them into bottomless pits.

If you said "not well," you'd be correct.

Olga, who was now ruling Kiev in the name of her three-year-old son, Sviatoslav, heard what her guests had to say and politely responded with something along the lines of "Okay, let me think about it. Return to your ships and await my decision."

The ambassadors, happy with this answer, went back to their boats. The next day, a large crowd of people from Kiev came out with big smiles on their faces, picked up the wooden ships, and carried the Drevlyan ambassadors on their backs all the way into the city. The Drevlyans, thinking this was a cool parade or something, kicked their feet up and waved politely to the crowd gathering inside the city.

Olga's men walked to the center of town and threw the ships straight into a twenty-foot-deep hole they'd dug during the night. Princess Olga of Kiev walked to the edge of the pit, looked down at the shocked ambassadors, and ordered her men to fill the hole in with dirt, burying the terrified Drevlyans alive under ten tons of dirt and rocks. Their grave has never been discovered.

But this hardcore princess was just getting started. Knowing that King Mal still had no idea what was going on, she sent a messenger to Drevlya to inform the king that yes, she would marry him, and that he should send his greatest warriors to Kiev so they could escort his future wife back to Drevlya for the marriage stuff. King Mal was so wrapped up in the "Princess Olga likes me" thing that he sent all his best troopers to Kiev without waiting for word back from his entombed ambassadors.

The Drevlyan warriors arrived at the gates of Kiev, where they were greeted by the captain of Olga's royal guard. The captain said that before these men could be admitted into Olga's presence, they needed to bathe in the royal baths of Kiev. The captain's men ushered the troopers into the baths, turned on the sauna, and then—just as Olga had commanded them—barred the door and set the entire structure on fire, melting King Mal's greatest warriors to death in the World's Hottest Sauna. Olga showed up to check it out and immediately started laughing her head off because, seriously, these guys would fall for anything.

King Mal, *still* unaware of Princess Olga's intentions, next received word from Kiev that the princess, along with all the Drevlyan warriors and ambassadors, was on her way to Drevlya for her Super-Happy Fun Marriage with the Man Who Murdered Her Husband. Her only request was that she be allowed to visit the city where her husband had died, and that a big feast be thrown to commemorate his death. Mal set it all up, preparing the best meats, cheeses, and mead in the Ukraine to receive his would-be queen.

Olga of Kiev rode out on horseback to the town, threw roses on the tomb of her husband, mourned his death, and then went to King Mal's party, where five thousand Drevlyan nobles and warriors fed her all kinds of delicious snacks and all the guests got their fill of mead and wine.

Then, once the party was raging and everyone was good and drunk, some Drevlyan guy had a moment of realization and was like, "Hey, Olga, how come none of your men are here with you? Did you ride all this way by yourself? And what happened to all those guys we sent to get you?"

It was roughly at this point that the doors to the banquet hall were flung open and a few thousand heavily armored Viking warriors came charging in, axes raised, screaming the bloodcurdling war cries of their Norse ancestors.

After wiping out another massive gang of her enemies, Olga of Kiev went on the offensive. Her army—all of whom had stayed fiercely loyal to their Viking princess—marched on the capital of Drevlya, surrounded it, and proceeded to starve the population into submission. King Mal, now sweating it, offered terms of surrender to Olga, saying he had no money but would do anything to get her Viking warriors to stop pummeling his citizens.

Olga thought about it for a second and then said she didn't need anything big—just something symbolic. "Bring me one flying bird from every household in the city and we'll call it even."

King Mal and his people were pumped. They brought her doves, pigeons, sparrows, ravens, and all kinds of other birds from the city. Olga accepted this offering, turned around, and marched back to Kiev.

When she was about a mile away from King Mal's capital, she ordered every man in her army to grab a bird, tie a slow-burning candlewick to it, light the wick, and set the bird free.

The freaked-out birds all returned home, where they set the entire city on fire, burning it to the ground and killing every single citizen. I like to imagine that Olga, like any good action hero, didn't even look back at the explosion as she walked off into the sunset.

Now, as you can probably tell, much of this background is rooted in folklore and legend. However, it can be said for certain, even among argumentative historians, that Princess Olga was one of the most capable rulers of the Viking era. She ruled justly and fairly and was beloved by her people throughout her time as regent for her young son, Sviatoslav.

Once Sviatoslav was old enough, he took over as prince of Kievan Rus, but he was gone on military campaigns pretty much all the time, and everyone in Russia basically saw Olga as their full-time queen.

So how did a mass-murdering princess become a saint? Well, in 957, Olga traveled by ship to Constantinople to have a diplomatic meeting with the powerful Byzantine emperor, and while she was there, she was so impressed that she

ended up deciding to convert to Orthodox Christianity. Emperor Constantine VII tried to get Olga to marry him and unite their kingdoms while she was there, but she had better things to do and said no way. Instead, she went back to Russia and immediately began building churches and converting her people to Christianity. By the time she finally died, she'd done so much for the Church that the bishops of Russia canonized her.

Saint Olga of Kiev

In 968, Kiev was besieged by a huge army of mounted warriors from a Turkic tribe known as the Pechenegs, who sneak-attacked Russia when Sviatoslav was out fighting the Poles and somehow made it all the way to the walls of the capital. Trapped in her beloved city with thousands of her subjects and her three infant grandchildren, Olga once again flexed her powers, ordering her men to resist and fight the barbarians at all costs, never surrender, never give up, etc. Then she came up with a stone-cold plan to get her people out of it.

First, she sent a messenger to swim the Dnieper River and link up with a small garrison of Russian troops stationed on the other side. This group of warriors was no match for the Pecheneg army, but Olga still ordered them to march right to the capital, blasting their trumpets and waving their flags. As soon as they came into view, the nearly eighty-year-old princess of Kiev threw open the doors of her city and, in full view of the enemy archers and soldiers, fearlessly walked toward the approaching troops with her arms out like she was going to hug them.

The Pechenegs, seeing Olga's attitude, thought the approaching garrison was actually the returning army of Sviatoslav, come to bust heads and destroy them.

They ran for it.

After they were gone, Olga sent an angry letter to her son, demanding he return and avenge this disgrace. He came back,

attacked the Pechenegs, and destroyed their chief. Happy to be avenged, Olga died of old age a month later and was given a good Christian burial. She was declared an Orthodox saint and Equal to the Apostles, making her one of only five women in history to receive the honor.

One of the grandsons she saved during the Siege of Kiev would grow up to become King Vladimir the Great, among the most famous and influential rulers in Russian history.

BLENDA

Speaking of terrible dinner parties, an eleventh-century Swedish legend talks about a sixteen-year-old girl named Blenda who threw a doozy. When she heard that Danish Vikings were coming while all the men were away on raids, Blenda rounded up the women of the village, cooked an awesome feast, and rode out to meet the marauding army with giant roasted turkey legs, huge hocks of beef jerky, and flowing mugs of delicious mead. The Danish horde basically walked into a huge party. Once all the men got drunk and fell asleep, Blenda and the women grabbed any farm implements they could find and killed the sleeping Danes with everything from shovels to riding lawn mowers. At least they died happy.

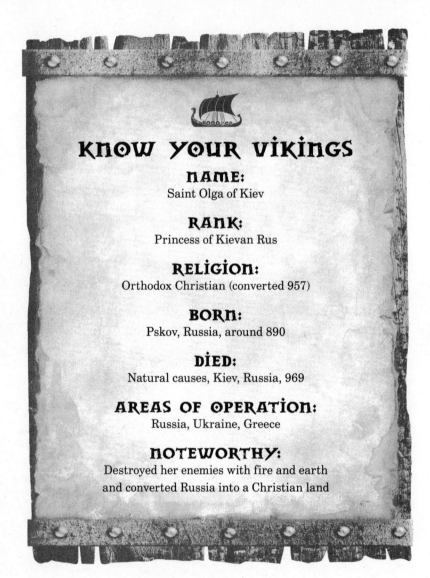

KNOW YOUR VIKINGS

NAME:
Saint Olga of Kiev

RANK:
Princess of Kievan Rus

RELIGION:
Orthodox Christian (converted 957)

BORN:
Pskov, Russia, around 890

DIED:
Natural causes, Kiev, Russia, 969

AREAS OF OPERATION:
Russia, Ukraine, Greece

NOTEWORTHY:
Destroyed her enemies with fire and earth
and converted Russia into a Christian land

ERIK THE RED

*A mass murderer persuades four hundred people
to follow him to Greenland
c. AD 980–1000*

> *Men will be more readily persuaded to go there
> if the land has an attractive name.*
>
> —Erik the Red

ERIK THE RED WAS A GIGANTIC VIKING
with a humongous red beard, a steady axe-swinging
hand, and a ferocious, white-hot temper that made him
completely fly off the handle and mass-murder his neighbors on
more than one occasion. He was banished from two different
Viking countries for being too over-the-top with his homicidal
behavior, and in his exile from civilized society he ended up
braving the uncharted wilderness of a previously unexplored
land. Then he came back home, somehow persuaded something

like four hundred people to follow him into the settlement of an unknown island that was blanketed by glaciers on 90 percent of its surface, became the ruler of his own private supervillain-style island fortress, and laid the foundation for the Norse people to discover the American continent roughly five hundred years before Christopher Columbus.

Erik's name comes from his red hair and fiery beard rather than his penchant for freaking out berserker-style and planting a hatchet in his next-door neighbors every time they forgot to return the lawn mower they'd borrowed. He first shows up in history around 980. According to the sagas, Erik and his dad had been forced to sail the seven hundred miles from Norway to Iceland after being convicted of "some killings," probably in one of the family blood feuds the Vikings were so famous for, and both men were forbidden ever to return. Erik, already in his thirties by this point, settled down in Iceland, bought a farm, raised sheep, married a woman named Thjoldhild (Erik's mother-in-law was even more awesomely known as "Thorbjorg the Ship-Chested"), probably went on a few Viking raids in the summertime, and did well enough for himself that he was able to afford a bunch of nice stuff like livestock, gold, jewelry, and slaves.

Things were going pretty great until one day some of Erik's slaves were messing around and accidentally caused a huge landslide that crushed a big part of Erik's neighbor's house with an avalanche of boulders and dirt. The neighbor, a little ticked off about this turn of events, clawed his way out of the rubble, got together a couple of his closest friends, and killed all the slaves with an axe.

Bad move.

Erik returned his neighbor's kindness by knocking on the dude's half-crushed door and then burying a sword in him when he opened it. That guy's cousin, a battle-hardened warrior known as Hrafn the Dueler, challenged Erik to a duel, so Erik the Red killed that guy, too.

The dead neighbor's kinsmen, wising up to the fact that Erik the Red was ridiculously ginormous and knew how to handle himself in an ultra-vengeance showdown, went the more civilized route and brought charges against Erik at the local Thing—the Viking meeting of townspeople to discuss laws and settle disputes. Erik was sentenced to lesser outlawry, meaning he had three years to get the heck out of Iceland, and that he wouldn't be allowed to return for three more years.

Now barred from Iceland and Norway, Erik the Red started gathering his stuff together and tried to figure out what the heck he was going to do. In the meantime, a neighbor of his named Thorgest asked to borrow some bench boards because he was having friends over for dinner. Erik, being the good neighbor that he was, was like, "Yeah, buddy, no problem, of course." Thorgest borrowed the benches but then forgot to return them. After a few months had passed, Erik went to see what was going on with those missing boards, and while he and Thorgest were having a civilized discussion, all of a sudden weapons were drawn and Erik found himself in a huge brawl in which he killed Thorgest's two adult sons and "certain other men" in hand-to-hand combat with a two-handed Viking long axe.

Erik found himself in Thing Court once more, and this time he was upgraded from lesser outlaw to full outlaw. This meant that he would lose all his land and property and be forced to leave the country immediately. It was also illegal for any Icelander to help him in any way, and any person from Iceland could just run up and kill him on sight without any legal penalty for doing so. The two families who had suffered because of Erik were pretty happy about this and immediately formed vigilante posses to hunt the dude down.

Erik the Red, for his part, was done with all this garbage. He was out of here. Civilized life was for chumps, anyway.

Erik got together his family, a couple of friends, a few slaves, and some livestock; loaded them onto a rickety old ship; and sailed as far away from civilization as he could get. Instead of heading east toward England, Denmark, or Europe, he went west in search of an uncharted landmass that had only been discovered about seventy years earlier—a huge, glacier-covered island we now know as Greenland.

Greenland had been accidentally discovered by the Viking Gunnbjörn Ulf-Krakuson, who found a "bleak land of ice" when he was looking for Iceland. Uninterested, and apparently realizing that this was a *different* bleak land of ice than the one he was looking for, Ulf-Krakuson turned around immediately and went back home. About twenty years after that, a guy named Snaebjörn Galti and a group of colonists tried to settle on one of the frozen islands off the coast of Greenland (known by then as "Gunnbjörn's Skerries"), but that didn't work out so hot. Living in Gunnbjörn's Skerries was so awful that all the colonists killed one another a few months after they moved there. The settlement was never heard from again, and nobody had even tried to sail near there in something like fifty years.

So you can see the appeal for Erik the Red.

Sailing for five days, Erik was hammered by storms, evaded *Titanic*-sinking glaciers in the North Atlantic, and rode out high winds and waves in a rickety old wooden boat. (Icelandic lumber was no good for shipbuilding, so all the boats in Iceland were used-car-style ships that had been built in Norway many years earlier.) The exiled Viking and his family made the perilous journey through uncharted waters to a landmass no European had ever set foot on. Erik found nothing of value on the east side of the island, but after he ventured around the cape on the southern tip, he found a few decent spots on the west side that would be perfect pasture for livestock. Erik settled down, unloaded his stuff, and prepared to live off the land with only his wits and strength to keep himself and his family alive.

Erik climbed mountains, sailed up and down inlets, discovered fjords and forests and green pastures, identified a few good places for settlements, and named almost every geographic feature on the world's largest island after himself. He survived three years in the hostile, freezing climate of Greenland, fishing for salmon and cod in the fjords, raising goats and cows in the fields, and constantly laughing his butt off because the native animals of the island had never seen people before, so you could literally walk right up to them and bop them on the head with an axe and then turn their bodies into everything from stylish fur coats to a delicious Sunday brunch.

While he was gone, Erik somehow managed to get his full-outlaw status downgraded to lesser outlaw (how he did this isn't clear, but it definitely involved another round of sword-on-sword combat with his old neighbor Thorgest). When he triumphantly returned to Iceland in 985, he had some amazing stories to tell people of how the glorious new land he had discovered was so completely radical that everyone should move there. Even though he knew the place was almost entirely covered by glaciers and solid ice pack, Erik told everyone he had named it Greenland because of its sprawling pastures and green fields. He was lying.

Inspired by his tales of adventure and his stories of a lush fantasy land where pretty girls and money and beer literally grew on trees, hundreds of Icelanders were persuaded to follow Erik back to Greenland and start a Viking colony there. Twenty-five ships loaded with men, women, children, and livestock set sail in 985.

By the time they reached Greenland, only fourteen of those ships remained—the rest had been sunk in storms, had crashed into ice floes, or had turned back because of rough seas and the sheer terror of the insane journey they were making. The colonists were a little disappointed with the scenery but stayed and settled in two villages. The main one, established at a place known as Eriksfjord (after Erik, of course), was home to nearly four hundred villagers.

The people of Greenland did pretty well for themselves. They hunted reindeer, wild hares, whales, and walruses; made contact and set up trade with the Inuit tribe; and established

trade routes with Norway, Iceland, and Ireland. The main Greenland exports were ivory from walrus tusks and narwhal horns, whalebone crafts, and exotic pelts and furs from previously unknown creatures like polar bears and Arctic foxes.

Even Erik settled down. He had three kids and built a couple of churches at his wife's request. According to the tales, he was "greatly annoyed" when she gave up the heathen gods and took Catholicism as her religion. He ruled over the Greenlanders as a jarl, solving disputes, running the show, and, as far as we know, not flipping out and killing anyone with an axe for some arbitrary reason. He did such a successful job of managing his colony (who saw that coming?) that more and more people moved to Greenland over the next few years. The colony thrived for nearly 450 years. It eventually grew to over three hundred farms, was home to roughly four thousand people, and had every Catholic religious structure ranging from a cathedral to a convent. It would fall apart in 1450, though, when a dramatic climate change made the land too cold for livestock and forced the Greenlanders to seek new lives elsewhere. Nowadays about 90 percent of the population is Inuit, and Greenland is run as a self-governing division of the Kingdom of Denmark.

As for the mass-murdering explorer/Viking hero, Erik the Red would rule Greenland for the next fifteen years or so. Even as an old man, he tried to accompany his son Leif Eriksson on an expedition that would eventually discover

North America (I'll deal with that story later), but while riding to the docks he was thrown from his horse, broke two ribs, and hurt his shoulder, so he wasn't able to make the trip to Canada. He died of illness around 1001, a man who went from violent outlaw to one of the greatest explorers and adventurers of the Viking Age.

DOES THIS LOOK INFECTED?

Medical care in the Dark Ages left a lot to be desired, and death was a common part of everyday life for the Northmen. Infections, fevers, tuberculosis, and other diseases were potent killers, and without important advancements like sterilization, running water, or penicillin, everything from a runny nose to a hangnail could potentially have ended up being fatal back in those days. Warfare was a constant threat, women died in childbirth with shocking regularity, and only the hardiest children survived their infancies. All told, the average life-span of a Viking was about forty years.

FERMENTED SHARK MEAT

One bizarre Icelandic delicacy is the famously horrible dish *hakarl*, which is made from the rotting carcass of a dead poisonous shark. Presumably ranking very high on the list of weirdest things ever eaten, *hakarl* is the meat of the Greenland shark, a creature so packed to the gills with acidic enzymes that eating it raw will literally kill you. In order to make this into something semi-edible, Icelandic torture-chefs cut off the shark's head, gut it, and then bury it in a shallow hole in their yards for six to twelve weeks. This is apparently long enough for all the acid to seep out of the meat, so once that's done the chef digs up the dead shark body, cuts it into strips, and hangs it up in his garage for the next six months or so. Once it's good and rotted and covered in a brown crust of grossness, the shark meat is taken down, cut into bite-sized chunks, and served at parties. *Hakarl* is available in some restaurants in Iceland, usually along with a printed warning that eating it "may cause gagging," and it is a traditional dish at Icelandic banquets during the midwinter festival Thorrablot. According to locals, it apparently goes great with the national drink of Iceland, *brennevin*, licorice schnapps cheerfully known as "the Black Death."

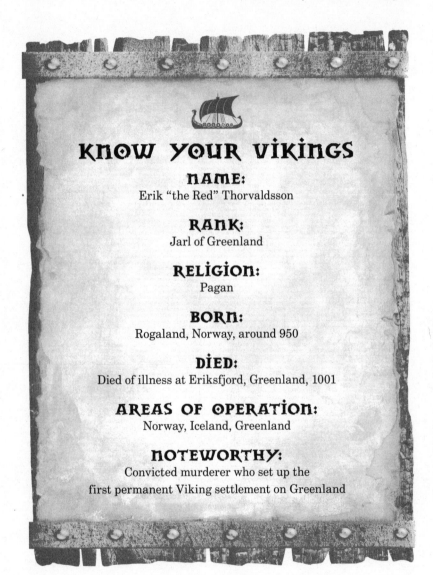

KNOW YOUR VIKINGS

NAME:
Erik "the Red" Thorvaldsson

RANK:
Jarl of Greenland

RELIGION:
Pagan

BORN:
Rogaland, Norway, around 950

DIED:
Died of illness at Eriksfjord, Greenland, 1001

AREAS OF OPERATION:
Norway, Iceland, Greenland

NOTEWORTHY:
Convicted murderer who set up the
first permanent Viking settlement on Greenland

THE VARANGIAN GUARD

The emperor of Byzantium's axe-swinging,
wine-swilling barbarians
AD 987–1204

It would be tiresome to recount the vicissitudes of this war; to narrate the cruelties which were perpetrated in detail would be disgusting; they can easily be imagined if one reflects that the Greeks, violent by nature and embittered by hatred, were frequently called on to exercise the right of retaliation, and they employed the rudest and most inhuman mercenaries for that purpose.

—Henry Smith Williams, *The Historians' History of the World*

KNOWN TO THE NORSE SIMPLY AS Miklagard, meaning "the Great City," the Byzantine Greek Empire's capital, Constantinople, was by far the largest and most impressive city in the Western world during the Viking Age. Bastioned behind an impenetrable set of triple walls, her landscape accented by gold-plated domes, towering spires, spectacular cathedrals, and bustling dockyards, the breathtaking capital of the Eastern Roman Empire was the center of the richest and most advanced civilization on earth. Inside the sprawling golden palace high above the city sat the emperor of Byzantium, an unbelievably powerful man who commanded a limitless treasury, an almost endless army of loyal warriors, and complete control over all he surveyed.

Keeping watch at every entrance to his palace, standing tall among the swirling Greek and Middle Eastern courtiers, citizens, and dignitaries, were men who didn't exactly fit in with their surroundings. Wearing sky-blue silk cloaks over their gold-plated scale mail armor, their red or blond hair falling down around their shoulders, their weathered hands clutching gold-embossed battle-axes, these terrifying battle-scarred warriors all stood well over six feet tall. The mere presence of their awe-inspiring beards and threatening axe blades was more than enough to keep order in the court.

These were the emperor's personal protectors, the Varangian Guard—combat-hardened, physically imposing Swedish, Danish, and Norwegian warriors imported from Viking Rus to defend the emperor with their lives against all threats foreign and domestic. Known as "the emperor's axe-bearing foreigners" (or, when they weren't listening, "the emperor's wine-bags"), the Varangian Guard were a mercenary army

brought in for their battle prowess and paid extremely well not only to guard the emperor but also to seek out his enemies and dispose of them as viciously and gruesomely as the Vikings saw fit.

The story of the Varangian Guard begins in 963, when a three-year-old baby named Basil assumed the throne of the Byzantine Empire. Since nobody in Byzantium really wanted to take orders from a toddler, a top advisor came in to help make decisions until Basil was old enough, and that guy brought in a Greek war hero named Phocas to put things in order. Phocas squashed out a potential uprising by a rival military commander, conquered some lands, and then refused to step down when Basil turned eighteen and was finally old enough to take over as emperor. Phocas basically told the teenage heir to the throne something to the effect of "Whatever, fools, I'm in charge now. What are you gonna do about it?"

What Basil did about it was secretly gather the support of the army, the royal administrators, and the people, launch a coup, and have Phocas arrested, stripped of his land and titles, and exiled from Byzantium forever.

After he took his rightful place on the Byzantine throne, Emperor Basil's first real problem came in the form of a bloodthirsty band of rampaging tribal warriors known as the Bulgars. A nomadic people who migrated to present-day Bulgaria from somewhere in Central Asia, the Bulgars had been united a few years earlier by a super-scary dude amazingly known as Khan Krum the Horrible. In the past decade or so, they'd defeated three Byzantine emperors in battle and turned one of their skulls into a decorative gold-plated wine goblet that they made Byzantine diplomats drink out of every time they came to discuss politics with the khan.

Krum the Horrible was long dead, replaced by the significantly less imposingly named Khan Samuel, and the new emperor Basil was getting a little tired of these guys pillaging and plundering Byzantine lands anytime they felt like it. Basil called up the full might of the Byzantine military, decked everyone out in top-of-the-line gold-plated gear, marched several thousand warriors into Bulgar lands, and charged head-on into the enemy formation, holding a gold sword in one hand and a huge flag depicting the Virgin Mary in the other.

He got his butt kicked. Hard. As in, pretty much every man in his army was slaughtered on the field, and he barely escaped with his life by running for it like a coward.

When Basil returned home to Constantinople, guess who was sitting on the throne?

That's right, our old friend General Phocas. As soon as that traitor heard of Basil's miserable failure, he came walking right back to Constantinople and told everyone that Basil was worthless, and all the soldiers and nobles of Byzantium immediately accepted him as the rightful ruler of their people and threw him a huge party with lots of cake and cooked meats. "Sorry, Basil, nobody wants to see your loser face around here again."

This, of course, just made Basil even angrier. And he was going to do something about it.

Raging like crazy, Basil headed north, and he didn't stop until he was face-to-face with King Vladimir of Rus. Vladimir, the grandson of Saint Olga, was the Viking ruler of Rus, and he of course had a massive army of hardcore Viking warriors at his disposal. But, incidentally, he was going broke after spending a ton of money on wars against the Slavs. Basil made Vladimir an offer: "If you convert to Christianity and give me six thousand Viking warriors to retake my throne, you can marry my sister, a Byzantine princess, and have a lifelong alliance with the richest empire on earth, and I'll send you a ton of gold once I recapture Constantinople."

As you can probably guess, the last thing General Phocas expected to see when he woke up one morning was a Viking onslaught of six thousand blond-haired, blue-eyed Swedish berserkers screaming toward him, their bloodstained axes and swords held high above their heads in attack position.

Basil and his Viking horde swept into Phocas's forward military base at Chrysopolis, stormed the walls, and killed every Byzantine warrior they could catch, wiping out half of Phocas's army in one afternoon of nonstop chopping. Then they went to Constantinople, forced their way through Phocas's defenses, recaptured the city, put the traitorous general to death, and spent the next two weeks locking up or whacking every Byzantine nobleman who had dared support the usurper.

Realizing that his own citizens were not to be trusted, Basil kept the six thousand Vikings on as his Varangians, meaning

Emperor Basil II

"sworn men." These hulking Norsemen would serve as the bodyguards of Byzantine emperors for the next five centuries, remaining loyal to their ruler not because of any patriotism or sense of honor, but because he was the one paying their salaries, and because he was paying them three times what he was paying any other warrior in the Byzantine military.

The six thousand Varangians were organized into twelve companies of five hundred men each. Each company was commanded by a Greek officer, and the entire guard was commanded by a Greek officer known as the *akolouthos*. This guy was so important that he got to walk right behind the emperor anytime there was a procession or a parade, which is a way bigger deal than it sounds. The guardsmen were stationed throughout the city, ordered to secure public buildings and entrances to the imperial palace, and called in as iron-faced Viking riot cops to break up everything from pirate attacks to fistfights between fans of different chariot-racing teams. They were equipped with the best weapons and armor in the Byzantine Empire, were decked out in the finest clothing, and earned two and a half pounds of gold per year, making them by far the highest-paid mercenaries in Byzantium. If they traveled with the emperor to battle, they were given the honor of being the first to plunder a captured city. It was a good deal for the Vikings all around, and when they returned home they were all super-rich celebrities. Plus the Viking women were

into it. According to the
Laxdaela Saga, when one
Varangian Guardsman
named Bolli returned
home, "his companions
were all wearing scar-
let and rode in gilded
saddles; they were all
fine-looking men, but
Bolli surpassed them all.
He was wearing clothes
of gold-embroidered silk
which the Greek emperor
had given him, and over
them a scarlet cloak. He
was girt with the sword
'leg-biter,' its pommel

now gold-embossed and the hilt bound with gold. He had a
gilded helmet on his head and a red shield at his side on which
a knight was traced in gold. He carried a lance in his hand,
as is the custom in foreign lands. Wherever they took lodging
for the night, the womenfolk paid no heed to anything but to
gaze at Bolli and his companions in all their finery."

The rowdy Varangians were also infamous for causing
trouble: getting into fights in bars, in gambling dens, or at

racetracks; drinking too much wine; and trying to make extra money by fighting wild animals in the coliseum. Even though they were pagans, they had to accompany the emperor to church on Sundays, and the only rule was that they weren't allowed to swear or sing while they were there, although one guy named Halfdan carved his name into the balcony of the world's biggest church—the Hagia Sophia— with a knife while he was bored during one service. It's still visible today.

Once the guard was set up and Basil's iron grip on the Byzantine throne was firmly established, there was still that whole thing to deal with about getting revenge on the Bulgars. Basil accomplished this in 1014, his Varangian shock troopers destroying the Bulgars' forces and capturing over fifteen thousand prisoners.

Basil decided to let his captives go free. But first he ordered his men to divide the prisoners into groups of one hundred. One man in each of these groups would get to keep one eye. The other ninety-nine in every group lost both.

The 150 lucky dudes with one eye remaining had to lead the rest of them home. When the procession got back to the castle, Khan Samuel had a heart attack and died on the spot. By 1018, Basil had conquered the entire Bulgar Empire.

From that point on, he became known as Basil the Bulgar-Slayer.

The Varangians would continue serving Basil until his death in 1025, and then would serve the emperors for the next two hundred years. They'd fight Fatimid Arab warriors in the Middle East, Persians, and Muslims; launch an invasion of Sicily; and once accidentally knock Emperor Michael VII unconscious after a night of partying too hard during his coronation.

THE VARANGIANS' LAST STAND

The Varangian Guard stood strong as powerful protectors of the Byzantine Empire for hundreds of years. They fought their last stand during the Fourth Crusade in 1204, when a big army of super-pious Catholic Crusaders took one look at Constantinople and figured, "Hey, forget the Holy Land—let's just destroy this place instead." The Varangian Guard went down fighting, defending the gates and holy sites and helping the emperor escape the city with his life, before finally falling under an onslaught of Crusader knights.

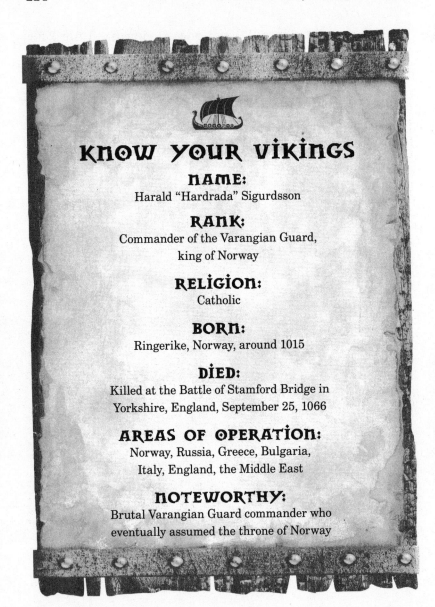

KNOW YOUR VIKINGS

NAME:
Harald "Hardrada" Sigurdsson

RANK:
Commander of the Varangian Guard,
king of Norway

RELIGION:
Catholic

BORN:
Ringerike, Norway, around 1015

DIED:
Killed at the Battle of Stamford Bridge in
Yorkshire, England, September 25, 1066

AREAS OF OPERATION:
Norway, Russia, Greece, Bulgaria,
Italy, England, the Middle East

NOTEWORTHY:
Brutal Varangian Guard commander who
eventually assumed the throne of Norway

CHRISTIANITY COMES TO HEATHENDOM

Olaf Crowbone baptizes the Vikings—
with violence
c. AD 960–1000

Olaf drove some out of the country, mutilated others
of hands or feet, or stung their eyes out;
hung up some, cut down some with the sword.

—Snorri Sturluson, *Heimskringla*

LAF "CROWBONE" TRYGGVASON IS THE
man typically credited with dutifully bringing
Christianity to the heathen lands of previously
uncivilized Northmen. Baptized at the hands of an English
bishop in a really fancy cathedral somewhere, the man who

brought the Lord's message to the pagans is still a legendary figure in Norway, a national hero, and a man so revered that many of the legends about his life read more like fairy tales than historical biography.

You'd think that all this would mean that Olaf was some kind of saint, wandering the countryside barefoot in white robes, high-fiving orphans, and turning rocks into bread, water, and fist-sized hunks of cooked beef.

He wasn't. He was a Viking. And even though Olaf brought Christianity to Norway and converted his people to the religion they still practice today, he didn't do it with olive branches, a soft smile, and a flock or two of white doves that shot out from the sleeves of his robes. He did it Viking-style— by terrorizing anyone who defied him with fire and steel until they understood the theological error of their ways.

Most of Olaf's superhero-esque backstory was almost certainly made up by later writers who wanted to make this guy sound even more awesome than he already was. But it's still such a good story that historians like to retell it as fact.

It starts around 968, when Norway was under the control of Harald Greycloak, the son of Erik Bloodaxe, who had violently taken over Norway after the death of the significantly less bloodthirsty King Haakon the Good. Closely advised by his famously evil mother, Gunnhild, Mother of Kings, Greycloak was told that the best way to cement his rule was to wipe out anyone who could ever threaten them in any conceivable manner.

Olaf Tryggvason's father, a minor Norwegian jarl named Trygve Olavsson (who was in some obscure way related to Harald Fairhair), was exactly the sort of man who could cause trouble for Greycloak and Gunnhild. The queen, in one of her purges, ordered a bunch of haters to stab Trygve to death in his sleep and burn his house down—not because he'd done anything wrong, but just as a preemptive strike to keep him from getting any bright ideas.

Trygve didn't survive his stabbo-burnination, but his pregnant wife, a Swedish noblewoman named Astrid, got word of what was going down and bolted as fast as possible with a small band of loyal followers. The expectant mother fled through the forest, stopping only to give birth to Olaf in a tiny hut in a marsh somewhere. Pursued by murderous agents of the queen for more than three years, the dedicated single mom protected her newborn child, escaped her would-be assassins, and made her way toward Russia to seek refuge with her brother, a *hersir* in the service of King Vladimir of Rus (Saint Olga's grandson).

Astrid didn't make it. Somewhere on the Baltic coast, the fleeing mom and her bodyguards were ambushed by slavers, and three-year-old Olaf was captured in the battle. The guy who captured him didn't really have much use for an infant, though, so he traded Olaf for a goat, because goats are way more useful than babies anyway. The guy who got Olaf quickly regretted his decision, however, and swapped the baby to some Estonian guy in exchange for a really sweet jacket. Olaf was raised in Estonia for the next six years, before finally being tracked down by Astrid's brother, who purchased Olaf's freedom and took him to the court of King Vlad of Kiev. Olaf was taken in, grew up with the Varangians, and learned important life skills, like how to sail a ship, how to do a lot of push-ups, and how best to cut people with a sword if you want them to die.

When Olaf turned twelve years old, he hunted down the slaver band who had imprisoned him, confronted them on the docks of a crowded city, and killed them all with an axe. Then, instead of facing justice, he just hopped the first longship out of town, turned Viking, and never looked back.

A mighty warrior with terrible manners and even worse hygiene, Olaf is famous for being one of the straight-up spine-crushingly meanest fighters in the combat-filled history of the Viking Age. His massive strength and fearlessness quickly earned him a legendary reputation unrivaled among Viking warriors of the time. During his early adventures, Olaf married a Polish princess, fought in the army of the Holy Roman Empire as a mercenary, circumnavigated the British Isles, and became so good at using the bones of animals to

prophesy the outcomes of battle that he earned the nickname Olaf Crowbone.

Of course, as I said, with many Viking stories it's important to keep in mind that we don't actually know how much of this is true. But it's still a good tale. And it's the only one we've got, so we're running with it.

What we know for sure is that Olaf Crowbone was Norwegian, spent lots of time in Kievan Rus when he was growing up, and became a heroic figure who by 991 had proven himself to his countrymen in countless raids across Europe. He first shows up in written historical records around then, when England was ruled by a man so terrible at responding to Viking attacks that he is known to history as Ethelred the Unready (or, if you prefer, Ethelred the Ill-Advised). Ethelred was a one-man screw-up factory who somehow found a way to take all the good things his great-great-grandfather Alfred the Great (he *was* pretty great) had done and completely botch them by giving the Vikings huge sums of silver every time they came around, like he was coughing up his lunch money.

So when Olaf Crowbone showed up in 991 at the head of a fleet of ninety-three black-hulled warships and ravaged the town of Sandwich of every last roast beef and PB and J he could get his hands on, the people of England knew that no military help was coming from their terrified king. Instead, one stalwart nobleman named Byrhtnoth rallied the people of the outlying villages, put together a ragtag militia to take on the Viking invaders, and did his best to bolster English spirits against the terrifying assault of Olaf Crowbone. Byrhtnoth was an incredibly brave fighter, but he also had an annoying code of honor, and after he surprised Olaf's troops on the banks of a river, he stupidly let the Vikings call "time out" so they could move their men into position before the battle. Byrhtnoth patiently waited for Olaf to march his guys across the bridge and form up into an impenetrable shield wall of Viking steel, and of course in the ensuing battle, the well-intentioned Byrhtnoth got the crusts cut off his ham-and-cheese by a berserking horde of trample-happy Norsemen. He was never heard from again. The poem about the Battle of Maldon (cleverly titled "The Battle of Maldon") is to this day considered one of the finest pieces of Anglo-Saxon literature ever written, but this was a small consolation to Byrhtnoth, who never got to read it because he was too busy being dead.

When King Ethelred the Unready heard what had just gone down with Byrhtnoth, he sprang into action and sent his fastest riders to the sea with a very clear message to deliver to the Viking invaders. And that message was this: "Here's ten thousand pounds of silver. Please stop killing us, okay?"

Olaf Crowbone took the cash. He sailed to Denmark, where he met up with the Danish king Svein Forkbeard, a man whose majestic facial hair was like the beard version of Harald Fairhair's long, flowing locks. Svein had seized power by overthrowing his own father, but the war had drained him of wealth a little bit, so when Olaf showed up talking about how the English king was giving out cash rewards for killing Englishmen, the two Vikings hopped into their ships and went back into action. In 994, they rolled up with a fleet of ships and burned Essex, Kent, Sussex, and Hampshire before laying siege to London itself.

Once again, Ethelred the Unready showed up with silver. Sixteen thousand pounds of it. Only this time, before letting Olaf go, he forced the Viking to convert to Christianity.

It was a conversion Olaf took incredibly seriously, and not just because he'd had some kind of intense religious awakening. Instead, he saw Christianity as a way to unify all of Norway under one common cause.

His iron-fisted rule.

Weighed down with a couple dozen tons of cold, hard silver and a thirst for glory, power, and fame, the already legendary Viking hero Olaf Crowbone sailed for Norway at the head of an army of English priests and battle-hardened Northmen who still hadn't had their fill of killing and torching things. He would stop at nothing short of reclaiming the throne of Norway and asserting his birthright as a descendant of Harald Fairhair.

On the way to Norway, Crowbone made a brief pit stop

in the Orkney Islands to test out his theory about the most effective ways to convert a staunchly pagan Viking population to Christianity. When he landed, he went straight for the jarl's house, captured the guy's son, and threatened to kill him if the jarl didn't convert. That worked. Then Olaf sent a message to the Norsemen of Orkney, telling them something along the lines of "Hey, you guys are all Christian now. Your Thor's hammer necklaces are now crosses, the Yule Festival is Christmas, and Odin is Santa Claus. Here are some churches. If you don't like it, I'm going to burn your houses down and chop you into bite-sized morsels with an axe."

That worked, too.

When Olaf Crowbone arrived in Norway a few weeks later, he found it in disarray. Harald Greycloak was dead; Gunnhild, Mother of Kings, was exiled; and power was in the hands of this guy named Jarl Haakon, whom everyone hated because he issued a lot of taxes and kept stealing all the other jarls' girlfriends. Crowbone crashed his ships into Haakon's fleet, bashed it into flotsam like it was made out of Popsicle sticks and toothpicks, landed on the shores of Norway, unloaded his crucifixes and battle-axes, and marched right for the capital. Jarl Haakon, running for his life, hid in a pigsty, where one of his ill-treated slaves stabbed him to death. And just like that, the twenty-seven-year-old instant-celebrity war hero Olaf Tryggvason Crowbone confidently sat down on the throne of Norway.

During his five-year reign as king of Norway, Olaf Crowbone set up the city of Trondheim, minted coins, and established a powerful centralized bureaucracy modeled after the English system. But what he's most famous for is his highly unconventional conversion of Norway from the Old Gods to Christianity. He did this primarily by threatening to torture and kill everyone who didn't convert. Subtlety and diplomacy just weren't his thing.

It's worth noting that despite all this, Olaf Crowbone still liked reading omens by casting bones, even though that's not really a super-Christian practice.

As brutal as his methods were, they were effective. So effective, in fact, that in addition to converting Norway, he also converted Iceland and Greenland, although in a much less bloodthirsty manner. With Iceland, he cut off all trade between his people and the Icelanders until they converted, refusing to send ships to heathen lands or to have heathen crews dock at his ports. The Icelanders accepted Christianity at the Althing (their annual parliamentary meeting) in AD 1000. With Greenland, he just had Erik the Red's son Leif Eriksson come stay with him for a couple of summers and talked to him about how awesome being a Catholic was. Leif converted, went back to Greenland, and eventually started building churches.

Despite his happy-go-lucky time dismantling pagan temples and hanging out with nuns, not everyone was super-excited that Olaf Crowbone was running things in Norway. Svein Forkbeard, the Danish king who'd had his sights set on conquering Norway anyway, joined up with his stepson King Olaf of Sweden and Jarl Haakon's son Erik, and together the three of them built a huge army and went to put Olaf out of their misery once and for all.

Olaf Crowbone sent out a call for troops, but his violent manner hadn't earned him a lot of friends, and when the combined navies of the Danes, Swedes, and Jarl Erik sailed into town, Olaf Crowbone had only eleven ships to meet them with. Badly outnumbered and facing an endless sea of Viking longboats, Olaf ordered his men to stand their ground. He personally launched himself into a ferocious last stand against impossible odds, hacking and swinging at anything that moved, in a battle frenzy that sent dozens of enemy warriors flying from the deck of his burning warship. He was last seen standing on the bow of the flagship *Long Serpent*, weapon in hand, engulfed in smoke and flames and swinging wildly as a horde of Danes swarmed around him.

Olaf's body was never recovered. Some legends claim he jumped overboard, swam to shore, traveled by land to Jerusalem, and became a monk. Others think he probably just drowned. It doesn't really matter either way. The most famous Viking in Norwegian history was never to be heard from again.

BLUETOOTH COMPATIBLE

Christianity was brought to the Danes by Svein Forkbeard's father, Harald Bluetooth. A warlike king who was famous for building an impressive string of fortresses to help defend his kingdom from rampaging Saxons in Germany, Harald Bluetooth was also the first Danish king to build churches and actively encourage the population to convert. According to the sagas, he converted in 970 when a priest named Poppo showed him the power of the Christian God by carrying a red-hot poker around in his bare hands. It was just a bonus that converting helped him make peace with the powerful Holy Roman Empire to the south and cut down on those pesky Saxon raids. Nowadays, Bluetooth technology is named after this guy, for some reason.

OH, RIGHT, THOSE GUYS

Sweden is the Viking country we know the least about because the people there were the worst at writing anything down. We know that for a long time, present-day Sweden was a series of small kingdoms made up of two peoples, the Gotar and the Svear. The first guy with the title king of Sweden was Olof Skotkonung, but a lot of folks have a sneaking suspicion that the kingdom was actually forged by Olof's dad, Erik the Victorious.

SAINT OLAF THE FAT

Olaf Tryggvason Crowbone is not the same person as Saint
Olaf, the patron saint of Norway, although it's easy to get the
two confused. Olaf Tryggvason was a descendant of Harald
Fairhair who successfully plundered the English countryside in
the 990s, returned home with a battle-tested army, claimed the
crown of Norway for himself in 995, converted his country to
Christianity, and was then attacked and deposed by King Svein
Forkbeard of Denmark in 1000. Saint Olaf, also known as Olaf
the Fat, was a distant descendant of Harald Fairhair, too (and
therefore a very distant cousin of Olaf Crowbone). Saint Olaf
successfully plundered the English countryside in the 1010s,
returned home with a battle-tested army, claimed the crown of
Norway for himself in 1015, continued converting his country to
Christianity, and was then attacked and deposed by King Knut
of Denmark (Svein Forkbeard's son) in 1028. Please be sure to
get them straight. There will be a test.

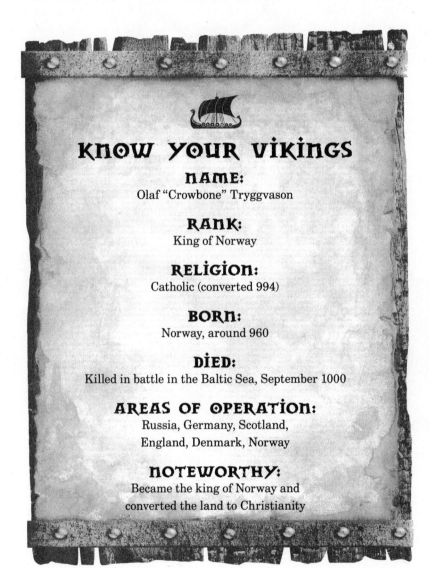

KNOW YOUR VIKINGS

NAME:
Olaf "Crowbone" Tryggvason

RANK:
King of Norway

RELIGION:
Catholic (converted 994)

BORN:
Norway, around 960

DIED:
Killed in battle in the Baltic Sea, September 1000

AREAS OF OPERATION:
Russia, Germany, Scotland,
England, Denmark, Norway

NOTEWORTHY:
Became the king of Norway and
converted the land to Christianity

THE VIKINGS DISCOVER AMERICA

Leif the Lucky and the Vinland expeditions
AD 1000–1020

> Leif set sail when he was ready; he ran into prolonged difficulties at sea, and finally came upon lands whose existence he had never suspected. There were fields of wild wheat growing there, and vines, and among the trees were maples.
>
> —The Saga of Erik the Red

DESPITE WHAT SOME OLD, DUSTY TEXT-books might try to teach you, the Vikings discovered North America 492 years before that slacker Christopher Columbus ever set foot in the West Indies. Even better, they weren't deluded into mistakenly believing they'd accidentally discovered India or China or whatever Columbus thought he'd bumped into; they knew they were in a land never before seen by European settlers. And when they engaged in hardcore tomahawk-to-axe combat with tough-as-nails American Indians who were a little less than thrilled by the prospect of a bunch of unruly Viking immigrants running around New England with battle-axes, they appreciated the awesomeness of it.

If the idea of a gigantic, bearded Viking berserker in chain mail armor charging a ferocious Beothuk Indian in full war paint doesn't get your blood churning into overdrive, I'm not really sure I can help you here.

The story starts back in Greenland, right around the time when Erik the Red was conning a bunch of gullible Vikings into relocating their families to an ice-encrusted island in the middle of nowhere. The average temperature was four degrees Fahrenheit in the winter, there were twenty-mile-per-hour winds, and there was enough yearly snowfall to bury your house. Apparently some guy named Bjarni Herjolfsson decided he should go visit his dad in Greenland, but as he was making the 450-mile trip from Norway through the North Sea, he was blown off course and ended up finding a huge landmass covered with trees and sand. Realizing this wasn't the desolate, miserable wasteland he was expecting, Bjarni figured he'd made a wrong turn somewhere, so he cranked the e-brake on his longship, popped a U-turn, landed in Greenland, found his pops, and was basically just like, "I guess I found some other new land or whatever, but who cares because hooray for Greenland, right, folks?"

When Bjarni told his story to Erik the Red, Erik's young son Leif was pumped. Like, super-pumped-up out of his mind.

Leif Eriksson pretty much thought about this new world every day for the next fifteen years, dreaming about the opportunity to win glory by discovering something important. When he was finally old enough, Leif tracked down Bjarni Herjolfsson, had coffee or whatever with him, and asked Bjarni to tell him everything about his voyage. Bjarni gave Leif a general idea of where this land was, and Leif was so on board with it that not only did he buy Bjarni's ship from him, but he also went out and hired several members of Bjarni's old crew so they could help guide him.

Finally, in the nice round-numbered year of 1000, Leif Eriksson assembled a crew of thirty or so rowers and explorers, loaded them into Bjarni's old ship, dusted off his trusty compass, and prepared for the adventure of a lifetime. Leif offered to let his dad, Erik the Red, lead the expedition, but as Erik was riding out to the dockyards he fell off his horse and was like, "Yeah, forget it. I think I'm too old for this stuff anyway."

Battling freezing windchills, terrifying storms, mighty waves, and every other horrible, ship-crushing hazard the ocean has to offer, the daring explorer Leif Eriksson plowed forward into unknown waters, first sailing all the way up the coast of Greenland and then making a sharp left turn, heading out into the frigid sea without any point of reference whatsoever. He traveled west for what seemed like an eternity, waves tossing his small ship around. He was determined to find the semi-mythical land of his dreams or die trying.

Then, after several days, he saw it. Off in the distance, on the western horizon.

Land.

He'd done it. Totally freaking out with excitement, Leif ordered his sails raised and told his crew to row as hard as they could toward this strange, puzzling landmass. From this point on, he became known as Leif the Lucky, because he was considered pretty lucky not to have sailed off the edge of the earth into the gaping jaws of some horrible Viking-eating fictional sea monster.

When Leif got to shore, he became the first European to set foot in the New World—an achievement that wouldn't be duplicated for almost five centuries. Standing triumphantly on what we know today as Baffin Island, Canada, Leif the Lucky struck a sweet pose and surveyed the landscape before him.

He quickly determined that this place was terrible. He named it Helluland, meaning "Slab Land," because it was truly just a flat, barren cesspit of ice and rock with nothing to offer him whatsoever.

But Leif the Lucky wasn't done. He got into his ship, turned south, and continued exploring the inlets and bays of the North American coast until he found something worth discovering.

The second place Leif reached was much nicer. Arriving in present-day Labrador, Canada, Leif cleverly named the region Markland, meaning "Wood Land," because, uh, there was a forest there. He also found some sandy beaches, went for a nice long walk, and then decided, "Okay, that was fun, now let's get out of here."

He continued south. And this time he hit the jackpot.

Leif the Lucky had finally arrived in a place he could write home to Mama about. Green meadows, a lush maple forest, beaches, warm weather, deer, rabbits, rainbows, and all kinds of other great things waited for him. If that wasn't enough, as his crews were exploring the land, a guy named Tyrker the German wandered off through a forest and accidentally discovered a huge patch of wild grapevines. This was such a big deal that not only did Tyrker the German start being known as Tyrker Grape-Finder, but Leif, in his typical Leif Eriksson fashion, named the region Vinland, which (as you can probably guess) means "Vine Land."

It was so rad that Leif decided to stay there for the winter. He and his men built turf houses, a smithy, a lumberyard, a

dock to fix their ship, and even a sauna to relax their tired rowing muscles. The Vikings picked a ton of grapes and made their own wine, which was huge for them because grapes don't grow in Scandinavia, and usually anytime the Vikings wanted a nice bottle of fine wine, they had to burn a Frankish monastery to the ground and pry it from the hands of a Catholic monk.

After spending the pleasantest winter of their lives chilling in Vinland, Leif and his men sailed back to Greenland and told everyone what had gone down. They were welcomed home as heroes, but there was also some bad news—Erik the Red was dead, and now everyone was looking to Leif to lead them as a jarl. It was a responsibility Leif couldn't refuse. He would never return to the New World.

That didn't stop his family, however, from taking up the reins and exploring Vinland further. Three more expeditions would make their way to the New World, each with varying degrees of success. First was Leif's brother Thorvald, who landed at Vinland and then possibly headed south to a second site. These early Viking explorers quickly realized, though, that the land they'd just discovered was already inhabited by native peoples. The Vikings didn't know what to call these tomahawk-slinging natives with the war-painted faces, so they came up with *Skraelings*, which was really just the default word the Norse used for fairies, elves, and pretty much anything they couldn't identify.

Well, these Skraelings decided they weren't huge fans of having Viking raiders patrolling their land, so they put together a war band and made a concerted attempt to forcibly evict Thorvald and his buddies by bludgeoning their faces inside out. Thorvald was killed by an arrow to the gut, becoming the first European to die on North American soil, and his buddies ran for it back to Greenland.

The next journey was undertaken a few years later by Thorfinn Karlsefni, a Norwegian trader who married Thorvald's widow. Thorfinn made an attempt to create a permanent settlement in Vinland, bringing a hundred or so men and women to Leif's camp and living there for three winters. While he was there, his wife, Gudrid, gave birth to their son, Snorri, the first European kid born in the New World. Thorfinn tried to make nice with the American Indians (probably either Micmacs or Beothuks), trading them milk and red cloth for furs and other items, but a mutual distrust, a dire shortage of red cloth, and the lack of any means of meaningful communication besides hand signs and funky dance moves eventually led to a series of battles between axe-swinging Vikings and hardcore natives. Thorfinn, with limited manpower, no supply lines, and no reinforcements, had to bail.

By the time the fourth Viking expedition to Vinland went down, the American Indians had seen enough. Not long after arriving, the Vikings were just looking for grapes, when all of a sudden, out of nowhere, these Skraelings came flying in from every direction, attacking with slings, axes, and other stuff. The Vikings started hauling outta there at top speed, but one of the Norsemen decided to make a stand and test the Skraelings' mettle: Freydis Eriksdottr, Leif's permanently angry axe-swinging sister. This no-nonsense Viking woman was pregnant and mad and didn't feel like running away from anything. She faced the fleeing Vikings and shouted: "Why do ye run, stout men as ye are, before these miserable wretches, whom I thought ye would knock down like cattle? If I had weapons, methinks I could fight better than any of ye!"

This didn't even slow the fleeing Vikings down, so Freydis took matters into her own hands. She grabbed a sword off a dead Viking and banged it against her chest Tarzan-style, shouting and daring the enemy to approach her. The

Skraelings who witnessed this fearless display got so freaked out that they immediately turned and fled. Freydis had saved the day, proving in the process that she had the iciest nerves of all the Vikings. She'd go on to kill five women with an axe in a dispute over grapes or something, an extracurricular activity that didn't win her a whole lot of friends when she got back to Greenland.

The Greenlanders continued to make occasional voyages to Markland to get timber, but after the Freydis mission in 1020, they pretty much gave up on ever dealing with Vinland again. Sure, grapes were great, but Vinland was about as far away as Norway, and it was populated by an unknown number of hostile people who resisted Viking occupation in a wide variety of violent ways. It totally wasn't worth it to mess around with them. Europeans wouldn't return for another four centuries.

The Vikings stopped worrying about Vinland; they didn't make many (if any) more trips there, and over time, it was forgotten about to the point where many historians wrote the Vinland Sagas off as works of fiction.

That is, until nine hundred years later, when confirmed Viking houses and artifacts were unearthed in Newfoundland, Canada, and scientifically dated to 1020.

PROVING THE DOUBTERS WRONG

In an effort to silence all the modern-day haters who said there was no way in heck that a Viking ship could ever make it across the North Atlantic, in 1893 a Norwegian dude named Christen Christensen built a full-scale replica of an ancient Viking longboat using the exact same tech Leif Eriksson had in the year 1000. Andersen sailed the ship from Bergen, Norway, all the way to Newfoundland. The trip took twenty-eight days and carried Christensen through freezing, dangerous waters, but he and his crew made it with little or no damage to their vessel. The ship that made the incredible journey was shown off at the World's Fair in Chicago later that year.

Replica Viking ship arriving in Chicago, 1893

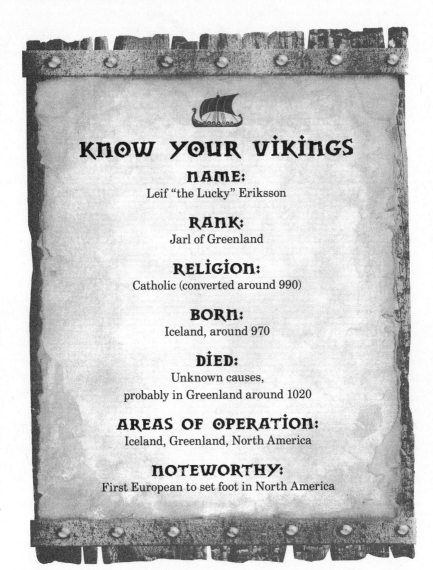

KNOW YOUR VIKINGS

NAME:
Leif "the Lucky" Eriksson

RANK:
Jarl of Greenland

RELIGION:
Catholic (converted around 990)

BORN:
Iceland, around 970

DIED:
Unknown causes,
probably in Greenland around 1020

AREAS OF OPERATION:
Iceland, Greenland, North America

NOTEWORTHY:
First European to set foot in North America

THE DECLINE AND FALL OF ETHELRED THE UNREADY

The Danish conquest of England
AD 1002–1035

In this great expedition there was present no slave, no man freed from slavery, no low-born man, no man weakened by age; for all were noble, all strong with the might of mature age, all sufficiently fit for any type of fighting, all of such great fleetness, that they scorned the speed of horsemen.

—The Encomium Emmae

◆

IN THE YEAR 1002, KING ETHELRED the Unready of England got really sick of the Vikings raiding his towns and torching his subjects to death, so he decided to celebrate the obscure festival of Saint Brice's Day by ordering the bloody execution of all Danes living in England. Across the land, Danes were put to the sword, burned alive in their homes and churches, and thrown into mass graves.

Among those killed in the Saint Brice's Day Massacre were the sister and brother-in-law of Svein Forkbeard, the Viking ruler who ripped the crown of Denmark from the cold, dead hands of his own father, terrorized England with flame and spear, and then sent Olaf Crowbone to a watery grave at the bottom of some harbor in Norway.

And Svein wasn't happy about having his sister and her family set on fire.

Svein went into a blood rage, got together a big army, and decided that the men of Denmark should head over and show Ethelred the Unready that ordering a Viking genocide is kind of a bad idea. By the time Svein was done, the crown of England would be firmly planted on the head of his son, a man who would rule England for twenty years as King Knut the Great.

We've already met Svein, but Knut's mother was no less intense. The Viking sagas refer to her as Sigrid the Haughty, and even though it's pronounced kind of like *hottie,* the dictionary definition of *haughty* is "arrogantly superior and disdainful," which is way more appropriate for a respectable Viking warrior-queen. Although now that I think about it, I guess *hottie* could also be applicable, mostly because Sigrid was infamous for getting lots of marriage proposals and responding to them by lighting her would-be husbands on fire. Aside from Svein Forkbeard, the only suitor who was man enough to be worthy of her was her first husband, King Erik the Victorious of Sweden.

You can probably imagine the kind of child those two managed to produce.

Knut was the second son of Svein and Sigrid, and since European custom ordered that kingship always passed to the oldest son, Knut was pretty much out of luck. He was groomed for war instead of politics and sent off to a secret island fortress off the coast of Poland, where he studied hand-to-hand combat with the Jomsvikings—an order of Viking marauders so over-the-top hardcore that historians can't determine whether they were real guys or just some ninth-century action-movie fan-fiction fantasy. Training under a massive Danish war-band leader called Thorkell the Tall, Knut mastered arts of war ranging from spear-throwing and swordplay to advanced tactical maneuvering and combat sailing techniques. Naturally, when Svein Forkbeard went off to war, this was the son he wanted by his side.

So in 1013, Svein and Knut arrived at the shores of England with one of the largest Viking fleets ever assembled—and this time, they weren't interested in plunder; they were mad, and they wanted blood. Ethelred the Unready, being a man deserving of his unflattering epithet, didn't know what to do. First he offered Svein money to leave. Svein refused. Then Ethelred offered money to *other Vikings* to help him fight against the rampaging forces of Svein and Knut. Norwegians like Saint Olaf the Fat came to England's aid, taking the cash in exchange for the opportunity to fight the Danes, but nothing could placate the Danish rage as they cleaved through Vikings, Norsemen, and Englishmen alike in their epic wave of destruction. Ethelred's armies were smashed. The archbishop of Canterbury—the most important religious leader in all of England—was killed at dinner after being pelted with food until he died. Knut, leading a side mission, forced a garrison to flee without a fight when he executed a bunch of English prisoners and floated their bodies ashore as a means of instilling terror.

Ethelred the Unready, seeing the end was near, did the kingly, manly thing and bolted across the English Channel for Normandy, leaving all of England at the mercy of Svein Forkbeard's marauding raiders. Svein considered crowning himself king of England, then suddenly died of illness. It was a turn of events so weird and unexpected that the English claimed he had been brought down by the spirit of Saint Edmund (the guy who got shot full of arrows by Ivar the Boneless's men a couple hundred years earlier).

With Svein's death, Knut was called home to Denmark by his brother Harald, who was now the king of Denmark. The second Knut left, Ethelred the Unready triumphantly sailed back into town, expecting some kind of parade, and he was all surprised when the English weren't really that happy to see him. They shook their heads at him disdainfully, took his crown, and proclaimed his son, Edmund Ironside, their king instead.

Naturally, this led to a civil war. Because it's not like the

English had better things to worry about, like what they were going to do when Knut came back to finish what he started.

The English fought each other, Edmund Ironside won, and then Knut came sailing back into town on a river of blood in 1016 and immediately picked up where he'd left off. Ironside raised an army of medieval knights and battled Knut for control of England. Ed put up a decent fight, but Knut and his Danish berserkers destroyed him at the Battle of Assandun, killing Ed and slaughtering much of the English nobility in the process. Knut took over the throne, crowned himself king, and, just to add insult to injury, went out and married Ethelred the Unready's wife, Emma of Normandy. Emma's grandpa was Hrolf the Walker, so you know she was down with Vikings, and she would go on to be the great-aunt of William the Conqueror, which owns.

Anyway, Special K's first order of business was to exile, execute, and/or imprison all Edmund Ironside's relatives and supporters, mostly because it's never a good idea to have people hanging around swearing blood oaths to avenge their friends' deaths. Then, despite the fact that this new king of England had come from a long line of people who made names for themselves doing terrible things, Knut established a twenty-year period of unprecedented peace in England. He basically went around to the different cities and counties building churches and merry-go-rounds and giving everybody high fives. He ruled fairly and justly and is now remembered as a pious and holy man, because he only assassinated people who deserved it, only took good Christian women to be his mistresses, and gave lots of gold to the Catholic Church.

In 1018, Knut's brother Harald died, and a bunch of Norwegians got all uppity and thought they could proclaim Saint Olaf the Fat the new king of Norway and declare that Norway wasn't part of the Danish kingdom anymore. Knut followed in his father's footsteps, the deposed king Olaf of Norway, and reestablished Danish dominance in Scandinavia. Then, just for good measure, he took over a couple of parts of Sweden as well, and by the time Knut visited Rome to hang out with the pope and celebrate the coronation of a new Holy Roman Emperor, he was already referring to himself as "King of All the English, and of Denmark, of the Norwegians, and Some of the Swedes."

Knut ruled for twenty years, eventually dying in 1035. We don't know exactly when he was born, but he was probably between forty and fifty years old. His kids took over his North Sea empire, but infighting and poor leadership doomed it to failure. By 1042, England was already back in the hands of Ethelred the Unready's other son, King Edward the Confessor.

We'll hear more about how that worked out for them in a sec.

GONE A-VIKING

Historians still like to argue about where the word *Viking* came from, but the best guess is that it's derived from the Vik, which is a bay on the southern tip of Norway filled with tiny islands that were perfect raiding bases for adventurous jarls. Regardless of its origins, during the tenth century, the term *Viking* was typically used only to refer to Scandinavian adventurers, pirates, and raiders who had "gone Viking" (meaning "gone adventuring"), rather than the entire population. Today, however, it's a general term applied to the civilization as a whole.

LONDON BRIDGE IS FALLING DOWN

The nursery rhyme (and Fergie song) "London Bridge Is Falling Down" comes from the Battle of London Bridge in 1014, when Svein and Knut tried to charge across the river Thames and attack the forces of Ethelred the Unready. Both forces met in battle on the bridge, but Ethelred's Saxons started to fall back, and before long Svein and the Danes were swarming across. Seeing the battle turning against Ethelred, Saint Olaf the Fat (who would later become king of Norway!), who was fighting on

Ethelred's side as a mercenary, rowed his longboat up to the bridge, tied a rope around one of the pillars, and then had his men row so hard that they pulled the entire bridge down, dropping hundreds of Svein's warriors into the mighty river below.

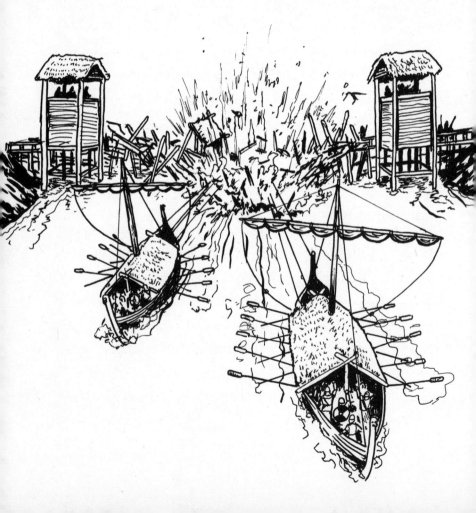

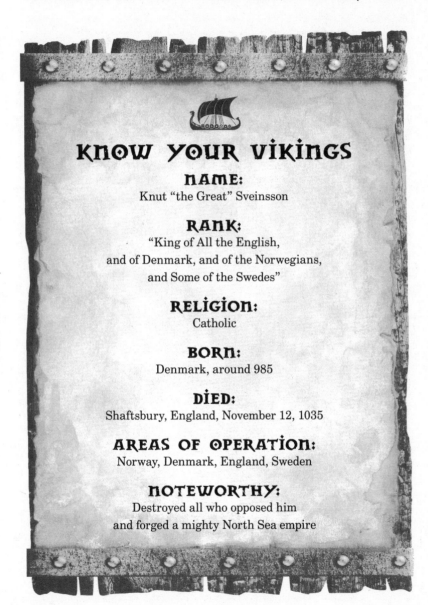

KNOW YOUR VIKINGS

NAME:
Knut "the Great" Sveinsson

RANK:
"King of All the English,
and of Denmark, and of the Norwegians,
and Some of the Swedes"

RELIGION:
Catholic

BORN:
Denmark, around 985

DIED:
Shaftsbury, England, November 12, 1035

AREAS OF OPERATION:
Norway, Denmark, England, Sweden

NOTEWORTHY:
Destroyed all who opposed him
and forged a mighty North Sea empire

THE VIKING KINGS

Keeping track of all this stuff can be tough, so here's a quick timeline with some of the more important kings of different places.

Reign Began	England	Norway	Denmark	Russia
827				Rorik
850		Harald Fairhair		
862				Rurik
871	Alfred the Great			
879			Godfrid	Igor
895		Erik Bloodaxe		
899	Edward the Elder			
934		Haakon the Good		
940			Gorm the Old	
945				Saint Olga
958			Harald Bluetooth	

Reign Began	England	Norway	Denmark	Russia
961		Harald Greycloak		
978	Ethelred the Unready			Vladimir of Rus
986			Svein Forkbeard	
995		Olaf Tryggvason		
1000		Svein Forkbeard		
1013	Svein Forkbeard			
1015		Olaf the Fat		
1016	Knut the Great			Yaroslav the Wise
1018			Knut the Great	
1028		Knut the Great		
1042	Edward the Confessor			
1046		Harald Hardrada		
1066	William the Conqueror			
1103		Sigurd the Crusader		

THE NORMAN CONQUEST

The Viking Age ends the way it began—with bloodshed
January 5–December 25, AD 1066

> Now when King Harald Sigurdsson saw this, he went into the fray where the greatest crash of weapons was, and there was a sharp conflict, in which many people fell on both sides. King Harald then was in a rage, and ran out in front of the array, and hewed down with both hands; so that neither helmet nor armor could withstand him, and all who were nearest gave way before him.
>
> —Snori Sturluson, *Heimskringla*

BY THIS POINT IN HISTORY, IT'S PRETTY safe to say that almost every single important person in France and England could trace his or her ancestry back to Viking ties somewhere. Sure, the kings of Europe weren't sailing around in longships whacking people in the head with axes, but somewhere in their family tree, they probably had a grandpa or two who enjoyed spending his weekends kicking peasants and plundering the countryside and a grandma who thought that was pretty cool.

But even though Viking culture was now finding itself getting all mixed up with cultures from everywhere else in Europe, the world was still waiting for one big event to finally tie everything together.

That would come in 1066, in the form of a Viking descendant who had fully integrated himself into medieval European Christian rule. And this mighty warlord would bring a stability to the monarchy that can be seen in England to this very day.

On January 5, 1066, the English king Edward the Confessor did a terrible thing: He died without leaving a son to take over. Edward, the seventh son of the now infamous Ethelred the Unready, had ruled England in relative peace for the past twenty-four years, with very few Viking raids and only a couple of wars against the Scots and Welsh. But with his death, the bloodline of Alfred the Great was at an end.

Upon his death, three men laid claim to the throne of England. They were all prepared to fight to the death for it in the most brutal manner imaginable, and the epic war for control of the country would change the course of British history forever.

The first man was Harold Godwinson, the most powerful

Anglo-Saxon earl in England. (If *earl* sounds a lot like *jarl*, it's because the English adopted the idea from the Vikings.) Harold's dad had been a jarl under Knut the Great, and his wife was Edward the Confessor's sister, plus Harold *swears* that right before he died, Edward was like, "Hey, Harold, you can totally be king after I die and there's no take-backs." The English nobles, who liked Harold because he was an English noble like them, said, "Yep, that works for us," and gave him the crown, and he put a big smile on his face and flopped down on the throne like he owned the joint.

This didn't really work for Duke William of Normandy. A direct grandson of Hrolf the Walker, William was Edward the Confessor's cousin, and he was all, "No way, dude, Edward *totally* said I could be king way earlier." (Apparently, being named king is like calling "Shotgun!" so you can sit in the front seat of a car.) William was the illegitimate son of a guy named Robert the Devil, who probably wasn't the nicest dad ever, so it shouldn't come as a shock that William ended up becoming the sort of duke who dealt with rebellious armies by chopping the hands off enemy prisoners.

The third man who wanted the crown was the ultra-heroic warrior-king of Norway, Harald Hardrada. Described as "the Thunderbolt of the North" and "the Last of the Vikings," Harald had the least claim to the throne but the most exciting backstory. A throwback to the old-school Vikings, this Norseman was a lot less interested in describing how he was

somehow distantly related to Knut the Great and more interested in just freaking out, planting his axe in everyone he
could find, and prying the bloody crown out of a lesser man's
cold, dead hands with a rusty crowbar.

Harald kind of ties together every chapter in this book
into one epic life story. A great-great-grandson of Harald
Fairhair, Harald Hardrada was the half brother of Saint
Olaf the Fat, who had led an attempt to claim the throne
of Norway from Knut the Great. At the age of just fifteen,
Harald was seriously wounded in the Battle of Stiklestad,
where the armies of Saint Olaf were crushed by Knut's Danes.

Harald fled to Russia, studied under King Yaroslav the Wise in Kiev (great-grandson of Olga), and then headed south to Constantinople, where he joined the Byzantine Empire's Varangian Guard. Rising through the ranks due to his noble birth and his ridiculous dual-axe-wielding battlefield blood-rage antics, Harald became the leader of the guard, charging into enemy formations and unleashing mayhem on anyone in his wheelhouse. Famous for ditching his shield and wading into the middle of battle with an axe in each hand, Harald stormed castles in Sicily, fought pirates in Greece, crossed blades with Muslim warriors in North Africa, and led a campaign that cleared the countryside around Jerusalem of a band of bloodthirsty bandits who had been preying on religious pilgrims. In 1040, he personally put down a Bulgar uprising with such ferocity that the emperor of Byzantium gave him the amazing nickname "the Devastator of Bulgaria."

After accidentally offending the emperor by making out with the empress (and subsequently escaping from a Constantinople prison by ripping the bars out of the windows, climbing down a sheer rock wall, and stealing a ship) and then marrying the princess of Russia, Harald eventually returned to his native Norway. The second he set foot on Norwegian soil, the Norsemen proclaimed him king of Norway (they'd already heard all about his amazing exploits like he was on a reality-TV show), and their support was so enormous that the guy who was supposed to be the actual king of Norway got scared and ran away.

As King Harald III (the first two were Fairhair and Grey-cloak), the Varangian-turned-statesman dominated Norway for twenty years, earning the nickname Hardrada, meaning "hard ruler." Which is awesome. He built churches, founded the city of Oslo (the modern-day capital of Norway), defeated the Danes in a couple of wars, ruled firmly but justly, and still spent his summers loading up longboats and personally going out on Viking raids because he was just hard like that. Now he had his sights set on adding England to his realm.

The stage was set for an epic, history-altering, three-way ultimate death match. In September of 1066, Harald Hardrada set sail from Norway with three hundred huge ships packed with foaming-at-the-mouth Viking warriors. William of Normandy also built a fleet of six hundred transport vessels to ferry his forces across the English Channel from Normandy to England. King Harold Godwinson of England was waiting for them both with an army of about fifteen thousand Anglo-Saxon warriors.

Harald Hardrada landed first, touching down in the northeast part of England near the former Viking stronghold of York. There he linked up with Tostig Godwinson, King Harold Godwinson's brother, who was willing to betray his own bro for a shot at power and glory and cool Viking helmets. The thunderous host of Norsemen marched to battle, crushing the combined armies of two Anglo-Saxon earls at the Battle of Fulford on September twentieth. Harald's men killed both enemy leaders in the process and then ravaged the countryside like they did back in the "good old days," when you had to destroy your enemies by marching twenty miles through the snow uphill both ways.

When Harold Godwinson heard about this, he took his entire army and raced out to face Harald, hoping to destroy the Vikings and get home in time to grab some dinner before fighting William of Normandy's armada. Harald Hardrada was not expecting to be dive-bombed out of nowhere by fifteen thousand screaming Anglo-Saxon warriors who had walked two hundred miles in less than a week. Godwinson caught Hardrada's army right around breakfast time, while they were still in camp, not wearing their armor, with most of their weapons and gear stashed on their ships.

As the English army advanced, a lone Norse berserker stripped off his shirt, asked his king for permission to die honorably in battle, grabbed a man-slaughtering two-handed Danish war axe, and stood astride the Stamford Bridge, which separated the Anglo-Saxon army from the scrambling Viking forces. The Anglo-Saxons, desperate to cross the bridge and strike the Norsemen, rushed the berserker, but this lone warrior single-handedly held the narrow bridge against the entire army of Anglo-Saxon warriors, killing over forty of the enemy and wounding dozens more in his bloody defense. He was finally slain when a Saxon soldier drifted down the river in a barrel and thrust his spear up through the planks

in the bridge, striking the battle-raging Viking in his lone weak point: his groin. The berserker fell, and the Anglo-Saxons swarmed over his body and plowed into the Vikings, who were still trying to get their act together.

The Viking king Harald, undeterred by the slaughter going on around him, grabbed a sword in each hand and waded through the enemy, dual-wielding death in a wrath-flavored berserker rage. After taking down several of the enemy, the fifty-one-year-old king was brought down by an arrow to the throat, and his army was massacred so badly that of the three hundred ships in Harald's invasion fleet, only twenty-three limped home.

But Harold Godwinson wasn't done dealing with Viking-related invasions just yet. Three days after wiping out Harald Hardrada, the English king received word that William of Normandy had landed his fleet on English soil. Godwinson raced back to the south, his army covering 250 miles, on foot, in less than three weeks. Then, just a month after facing Harald Hardrada, he met William of Normandy on the field of battle to settle the fate of England once and for all. They met at the Battle of Hastings on October 14, 1066, in one of the most decisive and epoch-changing battles in world history.

Historians aren't sure of the exact numbers, but we're pretty certain Harold Godwinson had more footmen and William of Normandy had more cavalry. Harold had the high ground, positioning archers and his elite bodyguard of housecarls (basically gigantic Anglo-Saxon axemen in chain mail who were organized and trained in the Viking warrior model) at the top of a hill behind a big shield wall of spearmen. William sent forward his spearmen first, charging up the hill as Harold's men flung arrows, stones, and javelins down onto them in a rain of pointy death. The infantry on the Norman left broke and ran, pursued hotly by a horde of Anglo-Saxon warriors, who broke ranks and charged wildly toward the fleeing Normans. William himself had his horse taken out from under him during some particularly fierce hand-to-hand fighting, and the Norman attack faltered. Undeterred, William sprang back onto his feet, took off his helmet to show everyone he was still breathing, and personally rallied his heavy cavalry into action. His armored horsemen barreled lance-first into the English lines, breaking them apart, and Harold Godwinson was killed in battle, surrounded by his axe-swinging housecarls, who fought bravely to the last man.

William of Normandy marched to London, was crowned King William I on Christmas Day in 1066, and was forever after known as William the Conqueror. He endeared himself to his new subjects by forcing any rebellious territories into submission, burning everything in sight, and salting the earth so no crops would grow. By 1072, all of England was firmly in the palm of his ever-clenched iron fist. William abolished slavery, absorbed the Viking Danelaw territory into the rest of England, added a bunch of French and Norman words

William the Conqueror

to the Anglo-Saxon language, built castles, and brought the feudal system to England, creating a British monarchy that reigns in England to this day.

William the Conqueror's accession marks the end of the Viking Age in England. There would never again be a mighty Viking raid on English soil.

CONFESS!

Edward the Confessor's nickname came from a title given by the Catholic faith to people believed to have lived a holy life. If you were a good man who stood strong for the Church but you weren't (un)lucky enough to die the death of a martyr, you were known as a confessor of the faith. It's basically one step below being a saint.

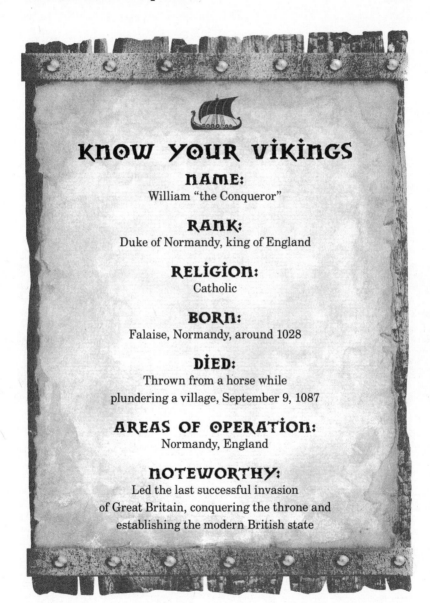

KNOW YOUR VIKINGS

NAME:
William "the Conqueror"

RANK:
Duke of Normandy, king of England

RELIGION:
Catholic

BORN:
Falaise, Normandy, around 1028

DIED:
Thrown from a horse while
plundering a village, September 9, 1087

AREAS OF OPERATION:
Normandy, England

NOTEWORTHY:
Led the last successful invasion
of Great Britain, conquering the throne and
establishing the modern British state

CONCLUSION

THE END OF THE VIKING ERA

> I've been with sword and spear slippery with bright blood. And how well we violent Vikings clashed! Red flames ate up men's roofs, raging we killed and killed.
>
> —Egil's Saga

DESPITE ALL THIS BIG TALK ABOUT **NORMAN** Conquests, berserker warlords, and epoch-changing invasions, the Viking Age in Europe didn't exactly end with one epic good-versus-evil sword fight to the death atop an active volcano with the fate of the world hanging in the balance. Instead, the Viking people, who were spread out in settlements from Kiev to Dublin, gradually began to settle down, mellow out, and start trying to act like civilized human beings for a change. They married nice locals, bought farms, raised families, and paid their taxes. They adopted Christianity, built churches, and went to Sunday school. Whether they were trading furs in Constantinople or fishing off the coast of France, they learned the local languages, adopted local customs, and gradually integrated with the civilizations around them. Before long, alarm bells screaming out warnings of an impending Viking apocalypse became a thing of the past.

But even though these guys were eating with forks and not killing people at the dinner table, nobody ever really forgot all the chaos they'd brought into the universe. In a very short period—a little under three hundred years—the Vikings had completely changed the entire Western world. The Viking homelands of Norway, Denmark, and Sweden had begun as a loose confederation of pillage-hungry warlords and emerged as three powerful European kingdoms that were big boys in international politics. In 793, England was an island divided into four kingdoms, none of which had ever heard of a Viking before. By 1066, it was a single, unified, powerful kingdom with a large Scandinavian population, ruled over by a guy who was descended from Vikings. Ireland had become completely intermeshed with Norse culture, which had brought plenty of wealth via trade, and the capital of the country to this day is a city founded by the Viking Turgeis the Devil. The entire northwest coast of France was called Normandy after these men, and was ruled by descendants of Hrolf the Walker. To the east, the town of Novgorod had gone from a small city-state dominated by the Viking leader Rurik to the beginnings of modern-day Russia. Viking trade had united most of the world by sea lanes, and settlements had popped up in Greenland, Iceland, and even (temporarily) the New World. Sure, the Vikings' methods were harsh and occasionally brutal, but by the time they were done, the map looked a lot more like it does today than it did when they started.

And that's not a bad thing to hang your axe on.

ACKNOWLEDGMENTS

The hungry battle-birds were filled
In Skye with blood of fowemen killed.
And many an island girl's wail
Was heard as through the isles we sail.

—The Saga of King Magnus Barelegs

THIS BOOK IS FOR MY WIFE, THE IRRE-
placeable Simone Thompson. I could not do any of
this without you. You are everything to me and I love
you with all my heart.

I'd also like to thank my family—Mom, Dad, Clay, Presley,
and John—and all my amazing friends for their endless support on this project.

Thank you to my incredible editor, Connie Hsu, and her
assistant, Leslie Shumate, for keeping me on track, advocat-
ing for the book, preparing awesome-sounding pitches, and
getting me pumped up to write this thing. And to my middle-
reliever editor, Deirdre Jones, who came on in the ninth inning

to earn the save, and who backed me up on the fact that you actually do crank a Super Soaker. You guys are great!

Thanks to my hardworking agents, Farley Chase of Chase Literary and Sean Daily of Hotchkiss, who bust a move so I get to write stuff like this. I am living in a fantasy world thanks to you.

And last, but not least, thanks to all the fans and readers of this series. Yes, that means you. I never cease to be amazed by the incredible support I get from all of you.

BIBLIOGRAPHY

> We rest the foundations of our story principally upon the songs which were sung in the presence of the chiefs themselves or of their sons, and take all to be true that is found in such poems about their feats and battles...no one would dare relate to a chief what he, and all those who heard it, knew to be false and imaginary, not a true account of his deeds; because that would be mockery, not praise.
>
> —Snorri Sturluson

Allan, Tony. *Exploring the Life, Myth, and Art of the Vikings*. New York: Rosen, 2012.

Anglo-Saxon Chronicle. Translated by James Ingram. El Paso, TX: El Paso Norte Press, 2005.

Baring-Gould, Sabine. *A Book of Folklore*. Charleston, SC: BiblioBazaar, 2007.

Belloni Du Chaillu, Paul. *Ivar the Viking*. New York: Scribner, 1910.

Berger, Melvin and Gilda Berger. *The Real Vikings*. Washington, DC: National Geographic, 2003.

Bradbury, Jim. *Capetians*. London: Continuum Books, 2007.

Buller, Laura. *History Dudes: Vikings*. New York: DK Publishing, 2007.

Claire, Israel Smith. *The World's History Illuminated*. St. Louis: Western Newspaper Syndicate, 1897.

Clements, J. M. *Lost Worlds: Vikings*. New York: Metro Books, 2012.

Clements, Jonathan. *A Brief History of the Vikings*. London: Constable & Robinson, 2013.

Craughwell, Thomas J. *How the Barbarian Invasions Shaped the Modern World*. Beverly, MA: Fair Winds, 2008.

Cross, Robin and Rosalind Miles. *Warrior Women*. New York: Metro Books, 2011.

De Pauw, Linda Grant. *Battle Cries and Lullabies*. Norman: University of Oklahoma, 1998.

Duczko, Wladyslaw. *Viking Rus*. Leiden and Boston: Brill, 2004.

Duffy, James P. *Czars*. New York: Barnes & Noble Publishing, 2002.

Duruy, Victor, et al. *The History of the Middle Ages*. New York: Henry Holt, 1891.

Egil's Saga. Translated by Bernard Scudder. New York: Penguin, 2005.

Eirik the Red and Other Icelandic Sagas. Translated by Gwyn Jones. New York: Oxford University Press, 1999.

Emmerson, Richard K. *Key Figures in Medieval Europe*. New York: Routledge, 2006.

Encomium Emmae. Translated by Alistair Campbell. Cambridge, UK: Cambridge University Press, 1998.

Evans, Andrew. *Iceland*. Guilford, CT: Globe Pequot Press, 2011.

Fee, Christopher R. *Gods, Heroes, & Kings*. New York: Oxford University Press, 2004.

Ferguson, Robert. *The Vikings*. New York: Penguin, 2009.

Forte, Angelo, et al. *Viking Empires*. Cambridge, UK: Cambridge University Press, 2005.

Fury of the Northmen. New York: Time-Life Books, 1988.

Grammaticus, Saxo. *The Danish History*. Melbourne: Book Jungle, 2009.

Gunderson, Jessica. *Vikings*. Mankato, MN: Creative Education, 2012.

Hall, Richard. *The World of the Vikings*. London: Thames & Hudson, 2007.

Haywood, John. *The Penguin Historical Atlas of the Vikings*. New York: Penguin, 1995.

Haywood, John. *Viking: The Norse Warrior's Unofficial Manual*. New York: Thames & Hudson, 2013.

Holman, Katherine. *The A to Z of Vikings*. Lanham, MD: Scarecrow Press, 2009.

Hopkins, Andrea. *Viking Explorers and Settlers*. New York: The Rosen Publishing Group, 2002.

Ibn Fadlan. *Ibn Fadlan and the Land of Darkness*. Translated by Paul Lunde and Caroline Stone. New York: Penguin, 2012.

Jesch, Judith. *Women in the Viking Age*. Rochester, NY: Boydell & Brewer Ltd., 1991.

Jones, Gwyn. *A History of the Vikings*. Oxford, UK: Oxford University Press, 2001.

Jones, Gwyn. *The Norse Atlantic Saga*. 2nd ed. Oxford, UK: Oxford University Press, 1986.

Kendrick, T. D. *A History of the Vikings*. Mineola, NY: Dover, 2004.

Leeming, David. *The Oxford Companion to World Mythology*. New York: Oxford University Press, 2005.

Light in the East. New York: Time-Life Books, 1988.

Lindow, John. *Norse Mythology*. New York: Oxford University Press, 2001.

Logan, F. Donald. *The Vikings in History*. Abington, UK: Taylor & Francis, 2005.

Lynch, John and Matthew Kelly. *Cambrensis Eversus*. Dublin: Celtic Society, 1852.

Macdonald, Fiona. *100 Things You Should Know About Vikings*. Broomall, PA: Mason Crest, 2010.

Magill, Frank N. *The Middle Ages: Dictionary of World Biography, Volume 2*. 2nd ed. London: Routledge, 1998.

Magocsi, Paul Robert. *A History of Ukraine*. Toronto: University of Toronto Press, 2010.

Margeson, Susan M. *Eyewitness Books: Viking*. New York: DK Publishing, 2010.

McKitterick, Rosamond. *The New Cambridge Medieval History*. Cambridge, UK: Cambridge University Press, 1995.

Miles, Rosalind and Robin Cross. *Hell Hath No Fury*. New York: Three Rivers Press, 2008.

Monaghan, Patricia. *Encyclopedia of Goddesses and Heroines*. Santa Barbara, CA: ABC-CLIO, 2009.

Moore, Thomas. *The History of Ireland*. Paris: Baudry, 1837.

Nilsson, Victor Alfred. *Sweden*. New York: P. F. Collier, 1901.

Nurmann, Britta, Carl Schulze, and Torsten Verhulsdonk. *The Vikings*. London: Windrow and Greene, 1997.

O'Connor, William Anderson. *History of the Irish People*. Manchester and London: J. Heywood, 1886.

Page, Raymond Ian. *Chronicles of the Vikings*. Toronto: University of Toronto Press, 1995.

Palgrave, Sir Francis. *The History of Normandy and England*. Vol. 1. London: John W. Parker, 1851.

Pearson, William. *Erik Bloodaxe: His Life and Times*. Bloomington, IN: Author-House, 2012.

Pushkareva, Natalya. *Women in Russian History.* Armonk, NY: M. E. Sharpe, 1997.

Roesdahl, Else. *The Vikings.* Translated by Susan M. Margeson and Kirsten Williams. New York: Penguin, 1988.

Rose, Carol. *Giants, Monsters, and Dragons.* New York: W. W. Norton, 2001.

The Sagas of Ragnar Lodbrok. Translated by Ben Waggoner. New Haven, CT: Troth, 2009.

Sandler, Stanley, ed. *Ground Warfare.* Santa Barbara, CA: ABC-CLIO, 2002.

Schomp, Virginia. *The Vikings.* New York: Franklin Watts, 2005.

"Secrets of the Viking Sword." *NOVA.* Season 40, Episode 1. Directed by Peter Yost. PBS, 2012.

Simons, Gerald. *Barbarian Europe.* New York: Time-Life Books, 1968.

Snorrason, Oddr. *The Saga of Olaf Tryggvason.* Ithaca, NY: Cornell University Press, 2003.

Stefansson, Jon. *Denmark and Sweden.* New York and London: G. P. Putnam's Sons, 1917.

Sturluson, Snorri. *Heimskringla.* Translated by A. H. Smith. New York: Dover Publications, 1990.

Sturluson, Snorri. *The Prose Edda.* Translated by Jesse Byock. New York: Penguin, 2005.

Tilton, Lois. *Written in Venom.* Rockville, MD: Wildside, 2000.

Traveler's Guide to Sweden. Stockholm: A. Bonnier, 1871.

Trueit, Trudi Strain. *Technology of the Ancients: The Vikings.* Tarrytown, NY: Marshall Cavendish, 2012.

Wallace, Robert. *Rise of Russia.* New York: Time-Life Books, 1967.

Walthall, Anne, ed. *Servants of the Dynasty: Palace Women in World History.* Berkeley: University of California Press, 2008.

Whittow, Mark. *The Making of Byzantium, 600–1025.* Berkeley: University of California Press, 1996.

Willcocks, Thomas. *History of Russia, from the Foundation of the Empire by Rurik to the Present Time.* Devonport, UK: W. Byers, 1832.

Wolf, Kirsten. *Daily Life of the Vikings.* Westport, CT: Greenwood Publishing Group, 2004.

Wooding, Jonathan. *The Vikings.* New York: Rizzoli, 1998.

Zenkovsky, Serge A. *Medieval Russia's Epics, Chronicles, and Tales.* New York: Penguin, 1963.

INDEX

Aachen, 172
Abbasid Caliphate, 24–25
Abbo de Saint-Germain, 150
Abd al-Rahman, 62, 70
Achilles, 69–70
Aella of Northumbria, 102–4
Aethelflaed, 118–19
akolouthos, 220
Alain Twisted-Beard, 172–73
Alcuin of York, 96
Alfhild, 147
Alfred the Great, 69, 108–17, 120, 230
America, Viking discovery of, 240–49
American Indians, 241, 246, 247, 249
Andersen, Hans Christian, 30
Angkor Wat, 23
Anglo-Saxon Chronicle, 1, 102
Armagh, and Turgeis the Devil,
    47, 49
armor, 13–14, 21
Arnor Jarlaskald, 108
Asgard, 32–33, 35–36
Asgerdr, 181–82
Askold, 78
Astrid, 227, 228
Athelstan, 139, 180
Atli the Short, 182
Aud the Deep-Minded, 144
axes, 12

Baffin Island, 243–44
Baldur, 38
Basil, 216–23
battle formations, 16
Battle of Ashdown, 110
Battle of Assandun, 257
Battle of Bravalla, 145–47

Battle of Clontarf, 52
Battle of Edington, 112–13
Battle of Fulford, 269–72
Battle of Hafrsfjord, 126, 128, 129
Battle of Hastings, 272–74
Battle of London Bridge, 259–60
Battle of Maldon, 231
Battle of Montfaucon, 159–60
Battle of Stiklestad, 267–68
Beowulf, 117
Bergonund, 181–82
berserkir (berserkers), 9, 15–16
Bjarni Herjolfsson, 241–42
Bjorn Ironside, 60–69
Black Sea, 74, 78
Blenda, 199
Blood Eagle, 103
bows, 13
Brian Boru, 52
British Isles, 25, 44–52, 277
    Alfred the Great and, 108–17
    reconquest of, 118–19
    Viking invasions, 44–52, 96–106,
        108–10
Brodir of Man, 52
Bulgars, 216–17, 222
Byrhtnoth, 230–31
Byzantine Empire, 24, 78
    Varangian Guard and, 213–23, 268

Camargue, 64
Charlemagne, 26, 161
Charles the Bald, 27, 62
Charles the Fat, 159, 161, 172
Charles the Simple, 160, 166, 168
Chartres, 166
China, Tang Dynasty, 22–23

Christensen, Christen, 250
Christianity, 42, 277
   Charlemagne and, 26
   Harald Bluetooth and, 237
   Hasting and, 65
   Olaf and, 225–26, 232–35, 238
   Olga and, 194, 196
   Rurik and, 78
Clonmacnoise Abbey, 49
clothes of Vikings, 90–91
Columbus, Christopher, 240–41
Constantine VII, 196
Constantinople, 24, 213–23
   Olga and, 194, 196
   Rurik and, 74, 78
   Varangian Guard and, 214–23, 268
Courland, 178–79
currency of Vikings, 94

dagmeal, 84
Danelaw, 106
Danevirk, 93
day in the life of Vikings, 84–85, 88
days of the week, 30, 41
Denmark, 125, 130, 135–36
   Harald Wartooth and, 28,
      145–46
Dir, 78
divorce, 88
Dnieper River, 74, 75, 77–78
Dorestad, 27
drakkar, 56
Drevlyans, 189–94
Dublin, 50–51, 91, 101
Dudo of Saint-Quentin, 59

East Anglia, 104–05
Edmund Ironside, 256–57
Edmund the Martyr, 104–5, 255
Edward the Confessor, 258,
   265–66, 274
Edward the Elder, 118–19
Egil Skallagrimsson, 175–85, 187
Egil's Saga, 175, 276
Emma of Normandy, 257
Erik Bloodaxe, 136–40, 143,
   177, 184
Erik "the Red" Thorvaldsson,
   201–10, 212, 241–42
Erik the Victorious, 237, 254

Erik Weatherhat, 125
Ethelred of Wessex, 109, 110, 118
Ethelred the Unready, 230–32,
   252–58, 259–60, 265
Ethelwold of Winchester, 118
Eyvind the Plagiarist, 130

félag, 92
Fenris, 40
Fimbulvetr, 39
flamethrowers, 60, 68, 78
Floki, 131–32
Fourth Crusade, 223, 266
Frankish Kingdom (Franks), 25–27,
   163–64, 172–73, 277–78
   Hasting and, 61–62
   Hrolf the Walker and, 164–71
   Siege of Paris, 150–60
Frederick VI of Denmark, 143
freemen, 11, 93
Freya, 36, 38, 41
Freydis Eriksdottr, 247, 249
futhark, 81

Galti, Snaebjörn, 205
Gandalf Alfgeirsson, 124
Gardar the Swede, 131
Garm, 40
Godfrid, 172
"going berserk," 15
Gorm the Mighty, 130
Gorm the Old, 125, 130, 135–36
Great Heathen Army, 99–105,
   108–10
Greek fire, 78
Greenland, 204–10, 241–42
Greenland shark, 211
Gungnir spear, 33
Gunnbjörn Ulf-Krakuson, 204–5
Gunnhild "Mother of Kings"
   Gormsdottir, 134–42,
     149, 233
   Egil and, 177, 179, 184
   Harald Greycloak and, 140, 142,
     226–27
Haraldskaer Woman, 143
Guthorm, 123–24
Guthrum, 105, 110–15
Gyda, 125, 128–29
Gylfaginning, 29

Haakon Sigurdsson, 142, 233
Haakon the Good, 130, 138–40, 226
Hagia Sophia (Istanbul), 222
hakarl, 211
Halfdan inscription, 222
Halfdan Ragnarsson, 110
Halfdan the Black, 123
Hamlet (Shakespeare), 186
Harald "Bluetooth" Gormsson, 95,
    130, 140, 142, 237
Harald "Fairhair" Halfdansson,
    121–29, 133, 136–37, 165, 176
Harald Greycloak, 140, 142,
    226–27, 233
Harald Hardrada, 224, 266–72
Haraldskaer Woman, 143
Harald "Wartooth" Hraereksson,
    28, 145–46
Harold Godwinson, 265–66, 269–73
Hasting, 59–69, 72, 115–16
Head's Ransom, 184
Heimdall, 40
Heimskringla, 134, 225, 264
Hel, 32
hersir warriors, 11, 13–14
Hervor, 148
hird, 11
Hnefatafl, 89
holmgang, 186
home life of Vikings, 83–91
horned helmets, 13–14
Hornklove, 122
horse-fighting, 89
Hrafn the Dueler, 203
Hrolf Kraki, 13
Hrolf the Walker, 163–71, 174, 257

Ibrahim ibn al-Tartushi, 83
Iceland, 176, 185, 205, 211, 234
    Erik the Red and, 202–4, 207
    founding of, 131–32
Igor of Kiev, 80, 189–90
Ingolf Arnason, 132
Ireland, 25, 44–52, 101, 277
Islamic Spain, 62–63, 64, 67–68, 70
Ivar "the Boneless" Ragnarsson, 69,
    101–6, 107

Japan, Nara Period, 23
jarls, 11, 126

javelins, 12
jewelry, 91
Jomsvikings, 254
Joscelyn, bishop of Paris, 151–57

keels, of longships, 55–56
Khmer Empire, 23
Kiev, 78, 80, 188–99
knarr, 56–57
Knut "the Great" Sveinsson, 238,
    253–58, 261, 267–68
Korea, Silla kingdom, 23
Krum the Horrible, 217

Lagertha, 147–48
Laxdaela Saga, 221
Leif "the Lucky" Eriksson, 209–10,
    234, 242–46, 250, 251
life-span of a Viking, 210
Lindisfarne, 1–3, 21
"Little Mermaid, The"
    (Andersen), 30
Ljot the Pale, 182
Loki, 37–39, 40
"London Bridge Is Falling Down"
    (nursery rhyme), 259–60
long axes, 12
longhouses, 85–86
longships, 21, 54–57
Lord of the Rings, The, (Tolkien), 41,
    92, 148
Louis the Pious, 26
lutefisk, 85

Máel Seachnaill, 50–51
Magnus Barelegs of Norway, 53
Mal of Drevlya, 190–94
Martel, Charles, 161
Mayan Empire, 23
"McVikings," 52
mead, 35, 36
Mercia, 104–5, 116
Midgard Serpent, 31, 37, 40
Minnesota Vikings, 4, 5
Mjölnir (Thor's hammer), 35–36,
    40, 42, 43
money of Vikings, 94
Moo of Insanity, 106
Moore, Thomas, 44
Moors, 64, 70–71

nattmeal, 85
nicknames, 19–20
Nidhogg, 32, 38–39
Norman Conquest, 264–74
Normandy, 168, 170–71, 277–78
Norse mythology, 29–41
Northumbria, 101–4
Norway, 135–37, 140, 142
   Erik Bloodaxe and Gunnhild,
     136–39
   Harald Fairhair and, 121–29
Novgorod, 75, 77–78, 80

Odin, 9, 15, 32–33, 35–40, 41, 43, 81
Odo of France, 151–60, 162
Olaf "Crowbone" Tryggvason,
   225–35, 238, 239
Olaf of Scotland, 180–81
Olaf the Fat, 238, 258, 259–60,
   267–68
Olaf the White, 144
Oleg, 80
Olga of Kiev, Saint, 188–99, 200
Olof Skotkönung, 237
Orkney Islands, 139–40, 142, 233

Pamplona, 68
Paris, Siege of, 99, 150–60
Patrick, Saint, 47
Pechenegs, 197, 199
Phocas, 216, 217–20

Ragnar Hairy-Breeches, 27, 60–61,
   99–102, 148
Ragnarok, 39–40
Ragnhild the Mighty, 128–29
Robert I, Count of Rouen. *See* Hrolf
   the Walker
Roman Empire, 24, 64–65, 213–15
Rome, and Hasting, 64–65, 67
Rouen, 27, 166
runes, 81
Rurik, 74–80, 82, 189
Rusila, 147
Russia, 73–80, 188–99, 278
Russian names, 80

Saint Brice's Day Massacre, 253
Saint Cuthbert Monastery, 2–3
Samuel of Bulgaria, 217, 222

Santa Claus, 30, 33
Saturn, 41
saunas, 91
sax knives, 13
Saxo Grammaticus, 145, 186
Seine River, 150–51, 152–53
Shakespeare, William, 186
shield-maidens, 145–47
shields, 14–15
shield walls, 16
short axes, 12
Siege of Kiev, 189, 197, 199
Siege of Paris, 99, 150–60
Sigfried, 151–59
Sigrid the Haughty, 253–54
Sigurd the Crusader, 70–71
Silk Road, 22–23
Silla, 23
silver, 94
Sinaus, 77
skalds, 19
Skofnung, 13
Skraelings, 246, 247, 249
slave, 74
"Snow Queen, The" (Andersen), 30
spears, 12
sporting events, 88–89
"starboard," 56
Stikla, 147
Sturluson, Snorri, 5–6, 9, 29, 281
   Heimskringla, 134, 225, 264
Surt, 40
Svein (Sweyn) Forkbeard, 105,
   231–32, 235, 238, 253, 255
Sviatoslav, 191, 194, 197
Sweden, 91–92, 237
swimming competitions, 89
Sword-Leif, 132
swords, 12–13

Tafl games, 89
Tang Dynasty China, 22–23
Thames River, 115, 259
Thing, the, 93, 126, 203
Thjoldhild, 202
Thor, 35–36, 38, 40, 43
Thorfinn Karlsefni, 246–47
Thorfinn Skull-Cleaver, 140
Thorgest (Turgesius), 203–4, 207
Thorkell the Stubborn, 146

Thorkell the Tall, 254
Thorolf Skallagrimsson, 176, 178–81
Thor's hammer (Mjölnir), 35–36, 40,
     42, 43
Thorstein the Red, 144
Tolkien, J. R. R., 41, 148
Tooth Fairy, 94
Tostig Godwinson, 269–70
trade, 91–92
trial by combat (holmgang), 186
Trondheim, 234
Truvor, 77
Trygve Olavsson, 227
tug-of-war, 89
Turgeis the Devil, 44–51, 58, 101
Tyr, 40
Tyrfing, 148

Ulfbehrt steel, 20–21
Umayyad Caliphate, 25

Valhalla, 33, 35
Valhalla funerals, 42
Valkyries, 33, 35, 36
Varangian Guard, 214–23, 268
Vidar, 40
Viking, origins of term, 259
Viking Age, dating, 53
Viking armor, 13–14, 21
Viking helmets, 13–14
Viking kings, timeline, 262–63
Viking longships, 21, 54–57

Viking mythology, 29–41
Viking nicknames, 19–20
Viking swords, 12–13, 20–21
Viking warriors, 9–19
     gear, 11–14, 20–21
     skalds, 19
     women as, 16, 145–48
Viking women, 134–35
     clothing and attire, 90–91
     day in the life, 84–85, 88
     raid duties, 16, 18
     as warriors, 16, 145–48
Vinland, 244–49
Vladimir the Great, 199, 218, 227, 228

warriors. See Viking warriors
Wessex, 105, 109–17
William "the Conqueror" of
     Normandy, 171, 266–67,
     269–74, 275
William Longsword, 171
Williams, Henry Smith, 213
women. See Viking women
World Tree, 31–33, 35, 40
wrestling matches, 89

Xuanzong of Tang, 23

Yaroslav the Wise, 268
Ymir, 30–31
York, 91, 139
Yule Festival, 33

DID YOU KNOW...

...a British Army soldier named Paddy Mayne once led fifty troops up a sheer cliff face with ropes and grappling hooks, attacked a fortress, captured seven hundred guys, blew up their coastal artillery, and then drank all their wine?

...the only female tank commander in world history, Guard Lieutenant Aleksandra Samusenko, took out multiple German Tiger tanks at the Battle of Kursk?

...an ammunition-toting bear named Voytek helped Polish artillery soldiers lob explosives at an impenetrable Nazi fortress high in the mountains of Italy?

LOOK FOR ALL THESE STORIES AND MORE IN
GUTS & GLORY: WORLD WAR II

TURN THE PAGE FOR A PREVIEW!

EIGHT HUNDRED HEROES

The Battle of Sihang Warehouse
Shanghai, Republic of China
October 26–November 1, 1937

> We will fight the enemy with our last bullet,
> and will punish him with our last drop of blood.
> Defend to the death.
>
> —Colonel Xie Jinyuan, Chinese Nationalist Army

THE CONSTANT CRACK OF RIFLE FIRE AND THE rumbling of armored cars echoed through the black smoke hanging in the night air. Shanghai, the fifth-largest city in the world, was burning. It had once been known as "the Queen of the Orient," a glitzy metropolis of high fashion, luxurious nightlife, bustling harbors, and towering skyscrapers. It was now rapidly being reduced to a mixture of bloody hand-dug trenches, empty bullet casings, and coiled tangles of barbed wire. The city of Shanghai had been home to three and a half million civilians. Now it was the front line of what would become the biggest and most destructive war in human history.

Amid the chaos and epic horribleness, Colonel Xie Jinyuan of the Chinese Nationalist Army calmly walked toward the imposing headquarters of his shattered division. The steel-and-concrete rectangular building known as the Sihang Warehouse was one of the few surviving structures amid the rubble of northern Shanghai. It was sturdy and secure; it backed against the Suzhou River and would be the perfect defensive position. Exhausted from three months of non-stop combat against a determined, unrelenting enemy, Xie Jinyuan decided that he and the surviving members of his command would make their last stand here.

A lot of uptight, pipe-smoking historians like to go on and on about how World War II started with Adolf Hitler's invasion of Poland in 1939, mostly because they don't think it's cool to pay attention to any history that didn't happen in Europe or the United States. In reality, the first shots of World War II were fired in 1937 when the swiftly growing empire of Japan decided to flex its bulging muscles by conquering everything around it. Fueled by its people's fanatical devotion to their emperor, their unequaled ferocity in battle, and some of the most advanced military technology this side of a science-fiction movie, Japan defeated Russia in a war in 1905, annexed Korea in 1910, and captured the province of Manchuria from China in 1932. In 1937, the Japanese war machine surged forward once again, this time with a full-scale attack into the heart of China itself.

The Chinese were in the middle of a civil war at the time, making it really inconsiderate of the Japanese to start bombing them while they were busy trying to kill one another. The uncoordinated, unprepared frontline armies of China were churned into mulch and lost their capital city, Beijing, to the Japanese pretty much immediately. By October, what remained of the Chinese military was falling back toward the Yangtze River and the important port city of Shanghai.

With more than a hundred thousand elite Japanese troops storming toward them, the Chinese prepared to dig in and defend their city at all costs. They had way more fighters than the Japanese, but they were not nearly as well trained or as well equipped. Shanghai quickly became a war zone, with defenders digging five-foot-deep trenches in the middle of streets while Japanese bombers reduced skyscrapers to smoking ruins. Homes were flattened, factories were gutted, and the biggest battle to grip Asia in over a century swept the economic heartland of China with fire and bullets.

By the time Xie Jinyuan moved his troops into the Sihang Warehouse on October 26, 1937, it was pretty much all over.

The Chinese had fought bravely, but they were outmatched in every way. A few days earlier, a flotilla of Japanese warships had pulled into the harbor, rained gunfire on the city, and then deployed hardcore Japanese marines right behind the main lines of the Chinese troops, all but cutting off their escape route. The command came down for the Chinese army to retreat from the city and evacuate as many civilians as possible in the process.

The specific orders given to Colonel Xie were simple: Hold the warehouse until someone kills you. Buy the civilians and soldiers of Shanghai time to get the heck out of there before the Japanese level the city into a giant pile of smoking misery. Make the invaders pay for every step.

Sihang Warehouse was the perfect spot to defend. Standing out like a beacon amid the destruction of the Battle of Shanghai, the six-story warehouse was made of bulletproof concrete and had plenty of good spots for sniper rifle hide-and-seek. Better yet, it was positioned across a narrow river from a part of Shanghai known as the International Settlement—a neighborhood that was home to British, French, and American embassies and citizens. The Japanese couldn't bomb the warehouse to cinder blocks with artillery and airplanes, because if just one little bomb missed its target and accidentally landed on some British guy's house, the Japanese would have an ugly international incident on their hands. They were going to have to take this warehouse the old-fashioned way if they wanted to get rid of Xie and his battalion.

Thirty-two-year-old Colonel Xie Jinyuan was a graduate of China's Whampoa Military Academy (later renamed the Central Military Academy), and the men of his battalion were some of the best troops the Chinese military had to offer. Kitted out with top-of-the-line German helmets, rifles, and other gear, these guys had been hand-trained by General Alexander von Falkenhausen, an awesome-looking old German military commander who had fought the British in World War I and had earned his country's highest award for military bravery. Xie knew he was outnumbered and outgunned and had no hope of reinforcement, resupply, or survival. But he didn't even flinch—he went right to work, preparing to give the Japanese the fight of their lives. He ordered his men to clear out the areas around the warehouse so they'd have open lines of fire. He looted surrounding warehouses and shops for food, ammo, and medical supplies. He rigged nearby buildings with explosives so he could blow them up if the Japanese tried to set up snipers or machine guns inside them. He had his men cut holes in the ten-foot-thick walls of the warehouse so they could shoot through them while staying behind cover. Sure, this was an unwinnable battle, but Xie Jinyuan and his soldiers were determined to show the world that China wasn't going down without a fight.

The Japanese arrived on the morning of October 27. The attack began at dawn.

The job of kicking down the warehouse fell to the soldiers of Japan's elite Third Division, who rolled up with mortars (potato-gun-looking tubes used to launch bombs short distances), machine guns, and armored cars. As the men of the Third Division approached the warehouse, they were greeted by a high five of Chinese bullets all up in their grills. Colonel Xie's troops were battle-hardened warriors, and they had spent the past three months defending a train station in the northern part of town. That battle had reduced their forces from 800 to 414, but the soldiers who remained were excellent marksmen and weren't about to freak out just because the Japanese were raking their warehouse with a nonstop stream of machine-gun bullets and other deadly objects.

The battle lasted most of the day, with the Japanese attacking many times. Colonel Xie ran up and down, screaming for his men to hold the line. At one point he even had to run downstairs with a bucket of water and a rifle because a couple of Japanese dudes broke into the warehouse and tried to set a fire in the room where Xie kept some of his bullets and fuel (which would have been pretty bad for him).

The Japanese attack halted that night, and Xie used the break to have his men rebuild the defenses and move their guns to different hiding spots. He even snuck a couple of his wounded men across the bridge to the British side so they could get medical attention.

The next morning, Xie looked out the window and saw an interesting sight—all along the British side of the river were people standing and watching the fight. British soldiers, international journalists, and even Chinese residents of Shanghai who had escaped to safety in the International Settlement were lined up to watch and cheer on the brave defenders of Sihang Warehouse.

One of the people lining the banks of the river was a girl named Yang Huimin. She watched in awe as the defenders spent yet another day fighting off nonstop attacks from the Japanese, shooting apart attempts to storm the building and raining down grenades and mortar fire on Japanese tanks that tried to roll up on the structure.

For Yang, only one thing was missing: The Chinese defenders didn't have a flag over their building. So that night, when the fighting stopped, she wrapped a Chinese Nationalist flag around herself, swam across the Suzhou River, and snuck into the building. By the next morning, Yang had already escaped back to the British side of the river, and the Japanese woke up to a giant Chinese flag staring them in the face. This made them even crankier.

For an incredible four days, the brave warriors of Sihang Warehouse held out against pretty much everything the Japanese Third Division had to offer. The 414 men (known to the international press as "the Eight Hundred Heroes" because Xie lied about how many guys he had with him) fought day and night, with no break from the constant Japanese onslaught. When the Japanese turned off the building's running water, the Chinese collected their pee in big gross buckets and used that to put out fires. When the Japanese put mortars and machine guns on opposing roofs, Xie blew them up with accurate mortar fire. When the Japanese drove tanks up to the front door of the warehouse, guys laid their lives on the line to attack them with hand grenades. When enemy teams broke into the lower floors of the structure, Chinese troops met them head-on with bayonets and face punches until the Japanese got out. For seventy-two seemingly endless hours, the Eight Hundred Heroes struggled for their lives, firing so many bullets that the barrels of their guns turned orange from the heat.

Xie had been ordered to defend to the death, but on November 1 his commanders told him to go—the city was evacuated and the mission was complete. So in the very late hours of the day, Xie had his men make a break for the river, leaving behind a few badly wounded soldiers to lay down covering fire with heavy machine guns. Xie and the 376 survivors of the battle reached the British side, where they would end up being confined for the next three years. For the first heroes of World War II, the war was over before it had really gotten started.

The Eight Hundred Heroes became superstars overnight. Despite the defeat at Shanghai and the destruction of the main Chinese military, the tale of Colonel Xie and his brave men inspired the Chinese people to carry on the battle and resist the Japanese takeover in any way they could.

PUTTING THE CIVIL WAR ON PAUSE

China was ruled by emperors for more than three thousand years, but when the last emperor of the Qing Dynasty was overthrown in 1911, there was a big, nasty debate over how the country should be run. This eventually blew up into the 1927 Chinese Civil War, during which a prodemocracy military dictator named Chiang Kai-Shek fought against Communist forces under Chairman Mao Zedong. When Japan rolled tanks and warplanes into town, the two Chinese leaders put aside their differences and agreed to stop shooting each other until they'd defeated the Japanese, and for the most part both sides held up their end of the deal. But after Japan was finally thrown out in 1945, the two dictators picked up right where they'd left off. Mao Zedong won the war and set up the Communist People's Republic of China on October 1, 1949. Chiang and his troops fled to the island of Taiwan, and the government they established there holds power to this day. Needless to say, China and Taiwan still pretty much mega-hate each other.

THE FALL OF NANJING

After the fall of Shanghai, the Japanese pushed farther south to Nanjing, which at the time was the capital of the Chinese Nationalists under Chiang Kai-Shek. The Japanese were not kind to the city. They killed everyone they found and looted and destroyed everything they could. Current estimates suggest that three hundred thousand innocent civilians were butchered in a truly horrifying display that causes trouble between the two countries to this day. Amid the carnage and misery, one man, a prominent Nazi Party member named John Rabe, used whatever powers he could to shelter people from the destruction. Rabe is credited with protecting as many as two hundred thousand people from Japanese brutality in Nanjing.

NAZIS IN THE HIMALAYAS?

On a weirder note, the Japanese invasion of China annoyingly messed up Nazi plans to travel to Tibet in search of a secret race of white-skinned supermen. Yes, you read that correctly. In 1937, a world-renowned German adventurer and zoologist named Ernst Schäfer went from Berlin to Tibet to explore the region and document its wildlife, ecology, and botany. But many folks aren't quite sure that's the whole reason he was traveling there. Schäfer was a pretty legit scientist, but most of the money for this trip was put up by Heinrich Himmler, the head of a super-nefarious Nazi organization known as the SS. Himmler not only saw this mission as an opportunity to put photos of heroic-looking, mountain-climbing Nazis on the front page of the news, but also is believed to have ordered Schäfer to search for anything from Indiana Jones–style magical devices to hidden races of white guys who had lived in the Himalayas for centuries. The British were pretty sure he was just scouting out the best trails to use to attack India from China, so they tried to block him from entering Tibet. But the enterprising German went around the Japan-China war, snuck past the Brits, and spent fourteen months climbing the Himalayas, gathering data and talking to the locals. Schäfer returned with journals packed full of notes on everything from Buddhist rituals to Himalayan wasp ecology, but he never mentioned anything about world-destroying ancient artifacts or Abominable Snowmen.

Type 89B Chi-Ro Tank Versus
Panzer Mark I

	Type 89B Chi-Ro Tank	Panzer Mark I
Type	Medium tank	Medium tank
Country	Japan	Germany (purchased by China)
First Produced	1928	1934
Length	18 feet, 10 inches	13 feet
Weight	14 tons	6 tons
Armor	17 millimeters	7 millimeters
Engine	120-hp Mitsubishi A6120V 6-cylinder	59-hp Krupp M305 4-cylinder
Top Speed	16 mph	31 mph
Crew	4	2
Armament	One Type 90 57mm cannon, two 6.5mm machine guns	Two 7.92mm machine guns

The main Japanese battle tank of the early war was basically a solid steel bunker on wheels with a machine gun and a little cannon mounted on top. The Chinese forces, on the other hand, had only a small number of German hand-me-downs that hadn't been cool for something like five years. Their small machine guns couldn't even punch through the thin Japanese tanks' armor.

HIROMICHI SHINOHARA

Expansion through China brought the Japanese up against the border of Russia, and in 1939 the Japanese and the Soviet Union had a short but insanely bloody war in the skies above the Mongolia-Russia border. Hiromichi Shinohara was a young, eagle-eyed cavalry officer who traded in his horse for a Nakajima Ki-27 Nate fighter plane, and he was such a master of air-to-air combat that he shot down four enemy fighter planes in his very first combat mission. Once he got the hang of it, he got *really* good, and on his second mission (the very next day) he became a fighter "ace in a day" by shooting down five Russian I-15 fighter planes in a single mission. Sure, the dinky old I-15 is one of those ancient-style Red Baron–looking wooden biplanes with the two sets of wings, and Hiromichi was flying a much more modern single-wing fighter aircraft with heavy machine guns in the wings, but it's still a pretty mind-blowing accomplishment.

Fighting among hundreds of diving, shooting, and exploding aircraft, Hiromichi engaged in scorching battles that more closely resembled Xbox Live multiplayer death matches than something you'd expect out of a real-life World War II battle. On June 27, 1939, he dove head-on through a 150-plane brawl and shot down eleven Russians like something out of an arcade game.

Hiromichi was awesome because his primary method of attack was to hold down the trigger of his twin-linked 7.7mm machine guns and dive from the sky at 300 miles per hour straight into the middle of enemy aircraft formations. Hiromichi's kill-or-be-killed, lone-wolf style would throw his prey into complete panic, their formation would break apart, and then he would go around shooting them one by one while they ran for their lives.

Flight Lieutenant Hiromichi Shinohara's entire military service career spanned just three months. In that short time, he managed to record confirmed air-to-air kills on an insane *fifty-eight* Russian fighter planes. He was last seen in August 1939, swarmed by enemy aircraft diving in on him from all directions. According to the report written about his death, the lieutenant managed to blow up three more enemy fighters before he was shot down and killed. He was the most successful Japanese Army Air Force pilot of World War II, and he hadn't even lived long enough to see the United States enter the conflict.